How to Read a Compass in the Dark:

Volume I of The Travels of Senator & Wendy V

- devised, compiled, written, typed, copyrighted, edited, produced, promoted, distributed, questioned, debated, recanted, and reinstated by Wendy V, 2006.

- cover photography and original musical score by Daver, 2006.

- any efforts to reproduce or sell any portion of this work without the author's express written consent will probably not yield much of a profit.

for Senator—

...until we are interrupted again...

Table of Contents

Introduction	6
Drizzled in Maple	9
Visions of Hubcaphones	15
The City That Never Sleeps	27
Elvis, A Star Trek Bride, and Lots and Lots of Doughnuts	37
"…And *Thank You* for Staying at the Ritz Carlton…"	53
Badlands, Good Rolls, and Some Really, Really, Big Heads	65
How I Became Rich and Senator Became Famous	85
Adrift	99
Afterword	123

Author's Note

For those of you monitoring my personal life, it should be noted that I have not run away with a politician. 'Senator' is, in fact, my dear, devoted David, a.k.a. Daver, a.k.a. Davy, if I happen to be indulging my Monkees fantasies. Long before we ever intended to be romantically involved (do you hate that phrase as much as I do?), we met in the workplace, where I had taken it upon myself to give some of my distinguished colleagues titles such as 'doctor', 'agent', and 'father'. Without much thought other than the syllabic rhythm scheme, I declared David to be Senator David Zuchowski. From our first conversation, he was simply Senator. After our first date, I awkwardly asked if I should start calling him by his real name, but he said that it would be weird. (Just for kicks I tried it once, and we agreed that it was just wrong.) So Senator he be for all eternity. I wish I had a better story for you, but at least now I can save myself the work of putting out a separate 'David edition' of the book.

~Wendy V
March 2005

Introduction

A Chinese philosopher (or, if not, he could have passed for one,) once proclaimed that a journey of a thousand miles begins with a single step. Profound. Very inspiring and such, but my journey of a several thousand miles began with a step into the music department of the bookstore where I worked and played.

It was in the spring of 2003, while plodding through the stages of a very necessary split up, that I remarked (mainly in frustration, yet still in enough seriousness to satisfy a re-emerging spirit of adventure,) to my close friend/mentor, "Well, if my life falls apart, want to go to Connecticut with me?" It was, of course, one of those utterances that you immediately wish to retract, fearing the discomfort of the recipient, or the embarrassment of the speaker. No one answered my prayers for a retrograde jump in the space-time continuum; however, my concerns were quickly alleviated when he replied, with characteristic grin, "Sure." I had forgotten this exchange until several months later, when we accidentally went to New England together. But I shall back up a meter or so.

Do not worry, patient Reader; this will not morph into any mercilessly tacky romance where junior high fantasies take on quaint settings with men who don't wear shirts and women who shouldn't. No, I promise not to invent any stripperlike pen names. No 'Rose McPassions' or 'Jade Nightblooms'. In addition, if you are still reading, I will not insult the wrinkling of your gray matter by delving into the details of his lightly flowing hair, or chameleon eyes… but just for the record, I could.

We spent our first month together shuffling between cars and coffee shops, daylight and moonlight, until one of us finally acquired a private residence. Such was the origin of our first 'travels' together. Events and feelings progressing as God,

Nature, and Disney intended, our days together soon grew into longer days together into double days linked by nights together. There is, I suppose, a point in every dating relationship when one must query of oneself how much of a good thing is truly tolerable. We decided to test this very question and plan our first out-of-town excursion together. Amidst the excitement and anticipation, I must admit I was somewhat apprehensive. Would this *companion de voyage* be able to stand me for six days straight? Would he run fleeing after several hours confined to the same four cubic feet of air space on a plane? Would he (politely, of course) suggest that perhaps we should each make other friends among New York's eleven million inhabitants? There was only one way to find out...

This is the first volume of the tales of our travels, beginning on a very dark day in August 2003.

~Wendy V
March 2005

Chapter 1
Drizzled in Maple: Mid-August 2003

Once we determined that we were both the type of people who liked to use every vacation day to the fullest, foregoing the 'Sabbath' day that some find necessary before returning to work, the plan for our first trip together was simple. We would spend Thursday night in Chicago, fly out to La Guardia first thing Friday morning, and return late Monday night. The primary object of our excursion was to introduce me to friends who I could no longer put off meeting. It wasn't that I never wanted to meet them; I was just nervous. *What if they don't like me and Senator returns home to find disturbing messages on his answering machine encouraging a break-up?*

We packed our bags Wednesday night and went to work the same shift Thursday so we could make our escape at 6:30pm. Not 6:40. Not 6:31. Around 2:00pm on the longest workday in history, we encountered rumors of a massive power outage affecting large chunks of the Northeast, including New York City. Mildly disgruntled, we caught reports whenever possible, which told us plenty of nothing in full useless detail. When 6:30 arrived, there was nothing to do but make our hand-in-hand getaway as planned. I suppose this must have left a coworker or

9

two with some juicy gossip, as most of the staff at the store where we worked were not privy to the fact that we were dating.

After a slightly disconcerting introduction to Polish food at Mabenka's Restaurant, (*my God, these people are huge!*) we settled into our hotel near Midway. Still unaware of New York's power situation ("authorities assure the public that today's blackouts were **not** terrorist related"), we called to check on the status of our flight. Everything progressing as planned? All right. Still on time? Good. Three obsessive alarm clock checks later, we were both asleep.

Two more calls in the morning and questioning several overworked ATA employees assured us that our flight was leaving on time. With plenty of time to spare, we claimed our places for prime napping in the appropriate terminal. A few minutes before our flight was to leave, the innocent ATA messenger announced that we would be indefinitely delayed. An hour? A day? Of course, no one seemed to know anything.

Situations like this group travelers into two distinct categories: those who quietly admit defeat and take their luggage home, consoling themselves with the revelation that it 'just wasn't meant to be', and those who say, "Hell no I'm not wasting four perfectly good days off in Joliet!" Initially though, we did not know which category each other fell into. With accommodatingly polite tones, we tried to read each other's mind. It was still early enough in the relationship to play the whatever-you-want-is-fine-with-me game. Finally, Senator bridged that treacherous canyon between honesty and compliance with a gentle, "Well, I wouldn't mind just going to New England instead... if you want to." The grin of a five-year-old on Christmas morning was my reply. We immediately bought tickets for the next plane to New England, landing in Providence, Rhode Island.

We had forty-five minutes to do everything over. Back to registration we ran. Then we headed back to the security check station with our brightest, most innocent, please-don't-hassle-us-even-though-it-looks-suspicious-that-we-just-changed-all-of-our-plans smiles. Security scrutinized us slightly, but passed us along uninterestedly. Soon we were on a plane to that closet of a state. There is something delightfully naughty about leaving the ground with the only other person who has any idea where you are.

What is there to do in Rhode Island? Not much if you do not yacht, so we rented a car and drove to the Eden of the East, Connecticut. Our first stop was a puppet museum run by a college. Tiny two-dimensional representations flirted with full-size Chinese costumed puppets. The European puppet theatre tradition is generally bastardized stateside, but for $2.00 admission, it was impressive.

That night we stayed in a beautiful bed and breakfast situated on lovely gardened grounds. In fact, the real melded with the surreal and brought the garden indoors with a ridiculous canopy of strongly flowered wallpaper looming over us, an umbrella over our every move. I really believed those stems and vines might strangle us while we slept...

It was also the night we discovered white pizza. While I had believed that it would be an alfredo concoction, it seems that 'white' is just an excuse to substitute more garlic for pizza sauce. The Frugal Gourmet once advised that, "Should you ever find yourself out on a date with someone, and you discover that he/she does not eat garlic, you should break up with the person immediately, because there is no hope for the relationship." So be it. We enjoyed our garlic pizza, and the comfort of a vampire-free evening.

The next morning began by driving Route 7 north, one of my favorite stretches of highway anywhere, not just because of the beautiful woods, streams, and villages, but also for the perfectly staged, yet nondescript graveyards that occasionally adorn it. Needless to say, it took a while to get to our destination. The Edith Wharton home in the Berkshire Mountains of western Massachusetts was our next stop. As a sucker for both good literature and good architecture, I paid the shameful entry fee and we began the austere tour.

What started out promisingly soon turned into a historically inaccurate commercial for local modern designers. As soon as we could ditch the duped group, we escaped to the serene and empty second floor, where we found a cozy chamber that flaunted a large window opening, with the glaring absence of a window. Laughing at the ridiculousness of the tour, and leaning out of the opening to absorb the fresh New England downpour, we did not notice one of the staff members enter. He suggested heavily that we come back downstairs. Dear Reader, I do not recommend that you spend your hard-earned money on this tourist trap. If you happen to be the ghost of Ms. Wharton reading this, I am so very sorry that I had to be the one to break it to you, but you should know what is going on. Perhaps a haunting is in order?

We drove on to Vermont, stopping in the even-smaller-than-Illinois'-Wilmington Wilmington. While some people accuse Vermonters of being aloof, I have always found them friendly. However, I will say that their attitude can be summed up thusly:

> "Welcome to Vermont. We are glad you are here. Please enjoy your visit and don't forget to sample our amazing cheeses and excellent maple syrup. (We made them here.) We would just like to remind you, though, that we are, in fact, from Vermont, and you are not. Have a wonderful holiday!"[*]

---

[*]This idea was clearly illustrated when we made a purchase at a local bookstore. When we presented a Barnes & Noble Mastercard, the unabashed cashier exclaimed, "Eewwww! Barnes & Noble!" After she recovered from the horror, she promptly denounced big business and chain stores in favor of small, private enterprises. This is certainly indicative of the pervading feeling of Vermont, and we would encounter this later elsewhere in the East.

Perhaps they are all just deported Canadians. Once you understand this greeting and proclamation, it is a magnificent state in which to travel. Every town is beautiful, and every town invented maple syrup. Our communion with this holy wine of the North occurred in a coffee shop/bakery where every item that was offered showcased maple syrup in some form: maple-frosted cupcakes, maple brownies, maple fudge, maple ice cream, maple candy, maple drizzled double maple mapleness. After making our divinely inspired choices, we sat down in the empty shop for a sugar-induced chat, only to be drowned out by the evening's entertainment. The lone acoustic musician plied his talents at an alarming volume, rendering conversation hopeless. I guess he was trying to make up for the obvious lack of an audience. At the first opportunity, we bolted out into the thickening fog to a vacant porch, maple wares in hand. With a significant Vermont-style maple sugar buzz, we walked back to our rustic inn for the night.

Continuing through Vermont, we traversed New Hampshire, stopping at several more graveyards and inventing the histories of many more previously vertical locals. By afternoon we were in Maine. The rugged beauty of Maine is unsurpassed. Even on the edge of civilized Portland, one is acutely aware of the rocky Atlantic's seductive presence. Not far from the city, our hotel was curiously positioned between the highway and a large, marshy area. After a simple dinner at the local café, (No, *really, he's a vegetarian. No, actually lobster is an animal,*) we returned to our room and fell asleep to the rhythmic pounding of the ocean.

Monday morning, sunny and warm without the despised humidity of home, brought the melancholy realization that tonight would be spent back in Chicago, and then Joliet. A firmly resolved pact was quickly established to make the most of the beautiful day before us. A drive along the ocean's highway led us to the Kennebunkport area, which was a little too thick with tourists. A few miles down from there, however, found us near a secluded rocky beach. As the sun and water fought for reflective rights, we scoped out the tempting rocks that would serve as our monstrous stepping-stones to the sea. With each venture further out, I wondered how long the tide would allow us to visit before it drove us back to the shore. As it turned out, the hospitable waves left us in peace for a few hours of silent rejuvenating bliss.

That night we drove to a small airport in Manchester, New Hampshire, returned our chariot, and danced our way down the moving walkways, which according to their endless warnings are eternally ending. Yes, we danced in the airport. I do not tell you this for the sake of a syrupy (100% pure) romantic ending, but to prove that there are still places in this world, even in airports, where fear is not the motivating factor and security relaxes… just long enough for a fine moment or two. In four days we covered six states, none of which we had originally intended to see. This is how we accidentally toured New England, and how I 'honored' my invitation of so many months before.

Chapter 2
Visions of Hubcaphones: Mid-September 2003

New York City, take two. Somewhere in the process of trekking through New England it occurred to us that: 1.) we were excellently paired travel companions (no whining, no blame assigned for wrong turns, etc.), and 2.) there was nothing preventing us from taking another trip that actually *did* arrive in New York City. Thus, our second excursion was set for mid-September, just one month after returning from New England.

Again, we would leave on a Thursday, making our escape at 6:30pm, as soon as our shifts ended. This achieved, we stopped for dinner at Pepe's Mexican Restaurant. Despite their claims, I would argue that Pepe's is not especially authentic to any particular region's cuisine, save Amerimex commercialand. In an excited mood nonetheless, we went to our hotel to pretend to get to bed before 10:00pm. Why we ever think this will work when we have to get up early is beyond me, given this plan's consistent rate of failure.

This time ATA lived up to its motto of placing us "on vacation", and we left the ground on time, bound for the original destination. Arriving at La Guardia Airport was a bit of a pleasant shock. How can one of the airports in a city of eleven million people be so tiny... and efficient? It may even be smaller than Chicago's Midway. Everything was clearly marked and made sense, which again, was almost too good to be true. This well-organized system is something that makes New York a very unique model city in the western hemisphere. Whereas Chicago and Los Angeles are cities designed for the motorist, New York has developed with the pedestrian in mind. They walk, and everything is designed from the pedestrian's perspective. If they do need to go long distances, they hop on the convenient and affordable subway. Contrary to popular belief, we found the subways to be quite safe as well. Hoofing it around town is far easier than most people realize, probably because they picture bodies smashed up against other bodies, nine out of ten of which are vying for the contents of your pockets. To date we have never experienced any of these problems, but there is an element of common sense involved as well.

Our first stop, naturally, was our hotel in lower Manhattan. To be more precise, we were staying in a hotel next to Donald Trump's building on the Chase Manhattan Plaza. Unfortunately, we did not happen across any of his spare change lying on the street, but fortunately, we also did not happen across him. I am not sure my fragile constitution could handle being in the presence of such raw materialism... and bad hair.

We found a small but satisfactory room way up in the thinning atmosphere of the fourth floor. Why is it that two people who never watch television at home suddenly become addicted to the Weather Channel whenever they enter a hotel room? We pack clothes for all kinds of weather, and we make plans that we carry out rain or shine anyway, so why the obsession with dignified and pretty anchorpeople predicting our temperate future? For the music, of course. It was in this very hotel room that I introduced Senator to the simple joys of the Weather Channel dance, or, should I say, I was caught unawares in an enraptured moment twitching my butt to the local 5-day.

When you are done laughing, Reader, and you are alone, try it. I promise you will not be disappointed, and the world may just be a better place because of it.

My nervous moment soon arrived. I have never been afraid to fly, assuming that if tragedy struck at 36,000 feet, there was nothing I could do about it anyway. Meeting your Essential Other's longtime friends, however, can be downright nerve-racking. Everyone wants the close people in their lives to get along and love each other as one big happy family. It is completely natural, but can also be unrealistically ideal. Everything I knew of his friends, Spencer-and-Michelle-from-New-York, seemed pleasant enough, but you just never know until you meet someone face-to-face. When I could stall no longer, we walked the block from our hotel to their fourth floor home. As it turns out, my imagined scenarios of awkwardness were in vain. These individuals are some of the most casual and uplifting people I have ever met. Plenty of 'New York smarts'; none of it flaunted. Plenty of funky fun; none of it obnoxious. Yes, they fall into that rare category of kindred spirits, as laid down by so many poets, writers, and musicians.

This evening's primary event was a walk over the Brooklyn Bridge to an Italian restaurant. For all of the cliches about the Brooklyn Bridge, one might think it is merely an overused image. No, Reader, I strongly suggest that you experience it for yourself if you get the chance... and bring a sweater. The bridge itself sports the highly recognizable gothic arches and spanning cables. Bikers and hikers share a great deal of space that is off limits to drivers. (Remember that this is a city for the carless.)

About halfway across, I turned around to take in the view of the Manhattan skyline. Most cities are breathtaking, especially at night, but New York is very alive, simultaneously in its past and present. You can feel, almost in a spiritual sense, the energy of a mini-world made up of the determined. Sound flowery? Let me explain. There is, and has been for well over a century, such a blend of cultures and minds that make up this city. People talk about minorities and warring ethnic groups, but there are so many different nationalities and heritages that make up New York, everyone really is in the same boat. There is a healthy mix of proud cultural identity and homey American patriotism. The public does not crusade to desegregate neighborhoods because they are not afraid of each other. There is not the racist whining that plagues Chicago and Washington D.C. because people are not categorized into vague and limiting color groups. Instead, they are Puerto Rican or Sicilian, Russian or Indian, Japanese or Ethiopian. Thus, there are distinct ethnic regions within the city, but they are generally celebrated rather than denounced. As I looked at the city from the bridge, I summed up my thoughts in the single statement, "I get it!" All of the songs and stories set amidst people's devotion to this city all suddenly made sense. Now, I was hungry.

Spencer, a chef at intervals in his professional life, and continually in his personal life, led us to the restaurant of an acquaintance, situated just inside Brooklyn. The night's weather cooperated (with the help of the Weather Channel's music, I am sure) so we could sit out in the giardino. My ravioli in a pea nage was delicious and plenty filling, but as the Midwesterner travels around the United States, he will notice a distinct difference in portion size.* After sampling traditional Italian desserts laced with cocoa, berries, and colorful drizzles, we lingered for quite some time, enjoying the conversation with the owner. Finally it was time to walk back to our hotel and say our goodnights to our friends.

---

*While you will not leave a New York restaurant hungry, you will not usually leave with leftovers. Dining at an Italian restaurant in the Chicago area, on the other hand, typically guarantees that you will take plenty home for at least tomorrow's lunch. Although, people in New York tend to be thinner than in many other American cities, so perhaps one should consider that fact as well.

Saturday morning was overcast (despite my sun dance), but not threatening enough to keep us locked in. The day's agenda was simple: walk around and do whatever we want. We began with an uptown sub ride to the Metropolitan Museum of Art. The museum was enjoyable, but not quite as spectacular as I had envisioned. It seemed a little limited compared to what I was anticipating. Yes, I fully expect this last statement to get me into trouble with a few New Yorkers. Sorry folks; we've got the Art Institute right here in Chicago.

Upon exiting the art museum, we took a short detour through Central Park. If New York is its own world, then Central Park is its own continent. Actually, the term *park* is rather misleading, as it covers several square miles. The best way to attack it is in sections, and probably in daylight, without a purse or wallet. Our rainy walk only took in a half hour's worth of trails before we ventured back to the main streets. Here we discovered a delicacy that was probably akin to common carnival food; however, it was new to us. Chilled by the dampness, we perked up to the smell of roasted nuts. New York streets have vendors everywhere, most of which are easy for the vegetarian to resist. The Nuts-4-Nuts stands, though, will not be ignored. Assorted nuts are roasted and then tossed in a honey and cinnamon concoction that demands the tongue's attention. After a bag, or two, we continued to make our way down Broadway, toward our hotel in the financial district.

When people hear that we stayed just a few blocks from the World Trade Center, they cannot understand why we chose to forgo this gruesome attraction. Neither one of us cared to stop or gawk, and in retrospect, I'm glad we didn't. It is basically a cement slab with a line of foreign tourists. Once you got up close, what would you do? Reflect on the fact that a lot of people died, a lot of property was lost, and a lot of lives were destroyed? We have all cried our tears and prayed our prayers; it is a horror upon which we do not care to dwell. In multiple trips to New

York we have never heard anyone there bring it up, and we are content to let it peacefully and respectfully lie as well.

Bypassing the World Trade Center brought us to an unexpected gem of the city. Just a few blocks from Wall Street and our hotel stood Trinity Church. This reddish-brown hued beauty looks as though it was plucked out of England, churchyard and all, and dropped in the middle of lower Manhattan, complete with a subway stop in front of it. The style is a sort of Victorian light gingerbread meets high medieval scheme. There are tall, narrow spires, trimmed with plenty of edging, and small crosses decorating tips and peaks all around. The yard is intertwined with a sidewalk that offers views all around the church, weaving in and out of the various architectural juts and courtyards. The crowning glory, ironically, lies at the foot of the church in its graveyard. Facing a major street, with taxis and pedestrians passing indifferently, hundreds of former New Yorkers, some born in the eighteenth century, rest under traditional tablet-style stones. Some contain religious poems or words of encouragement and resurrection. Others hold images of skulls with wings protruding from the sides, a throwback to the medieval *danse macabre.* My favorites were the ones that seemed to reprimand the onlooker with reminders of life's brevity. Their warnings, though somber, still displayed an almost impish flavor. After reading dozens of epitaphs of silent hosts, we parted from the departed.

Saturday evening we took in a jazz concert at the famous Blue Note. Though I have a very limited knowledge and understanding of jazz, it really is the defining soundtrack of New York. The complete jazz club experience, though lacking some of the glamour of yesteryear, includes dressing up, waiting outside in a wrap-around line, cramming into a small, older-than-your-grandpa venue, and letting the music (and your drink if you are so inclined) take you deep into your own imagination. We waited for twenty or thirty minutes in line, with some unplanned 'entertainment'.

The local Blue Note Homeless Guy should be given credit for his various money begging tactics. He first asked if we had any of his cds, ready to 'sell' us some. I ignored him; my sweet partner politely answered, "No. No, thanks." When it became clear that we were not interested, he moved on... or so we thought. He later combed the line, hat in hand, with, "I'm homeless. Give me a dollar." At the time I was, for various reasons, living between three houses, so I replied, "*I'm* homeless. Give *me* a dollar!" Again, his leave was only temporary. The third time that he approached us asking for money, I stared at him blankly. "*Oh, je suis desole. Je ne comprend pas d'anglais. Nous sommes francais, mais nous aimons New York!*"* I think he finally got the hint.

Once inside, we were seated as couples across from each other at a table that literally butted up against the stage. After some quick bargaining with the next couple, we were able to sit together comfortably, just a few feet from the band. The music flirted with simple melodies and complex free improvisation the way I would imagine that great jazz should. I was immediately lost in a whirlwind of musical movement. Another surprise was the amazing skill of the drummer. Jeff Tain Watts is a well-kept secret that deserves to be blabbed. His skill stole the show. My only regret that night is that there was no room to dance.

Sunday morning we set out on foot for Greenwich Village. A friend tipped Senator off to several record stores in the area, and I just wanted to see what all the artistic fuss of Greenwich was about. One success, one failure. We found many record stores of various calibers. Not particularly wanting to purchase anything, my favorite stores were the ones whose messes were contained in run down shops of bygone eras. While Senator scoped the merchandise, I checked out the tin ceilings and battered original woodwork. I cannot help it; I am too

---

*"Oh, I'm sorry. I don't understand English. We are French, but we love New York!"

romantically curious about the history of buildings and their inhabitants. Just about the time I have the fictitious details of characters who once owned these stores worked out, it is time to go.

The 'failure' that I mentioned refers to all of this nonsense about Greenwich being an artistic haven. Perhaps it once was, but now it is pretty much a large neighborhood with lots of plants and viny greenery, and an Italian restaurant or cappuccino bar on every corner. (Not that that's a bad thing!) In fact, it was while meandering around the Italian flavored streets that we discovered Murray's, the world's greatest cheese shop, and an essential component of all future visits we would make to New York City.

Murray's is a real cheese shop. They sell a few other accompaniments, such as pesto spreads or flatbread crackers, but cheese is their divine purpose of existence. As other people maneuvered in the line of the tiny shop to place their orders, we paced back and forth in front of the endless display case like wolves choosing between Irish cheddar sheep and marinated Italian boccacini lambs. When we had finally made our cholesterol-heavy decision, we claimed our place on the ancient bench in front of the store, instantly becoming a living commercial for Murray's. In six days God created the world and man. On the seventh day he rested. On the eighth day, when he was well rested, he created cheese.

Later that evening we met Spencer and Michelle for another jazz concert. Henry Threadgill, whom even *I* had heard of, was to perform some newer work in a small venue. The advertisement listed the 'hubcaphone' as the featured instrument of the night. Before you bow your head in shame, dear Reader, I will comfort you by telling you that you are among six billion other people who have never heard of the hubcaphone. After some theorizing, we realized that the hubcaphone was an original contraption made out of hubcaps. Much to our chagrin, the instrument was not present at the actual performance.

Recordings of the car-part-turned-jazz-instrument were our only glimpses of its clanging mystique. The concert was enjoyable, but the real entertainment was the many uses we developed throughout the evening for the word 'hubcaphone'. *What the hubcaphone is going on here? Excuse me; I have to use the hubcaphone. He's nothin' but a big hubcaphoney! Whatdya say you n me hook up for a little hubcaphone action?* We rounded out our splendidly juvenile silliness with an ice cream cone at a local, and of course, historically established, ice cream shop, where, we were told, JFK Jr. used to hang out.

  The next day was filled with more wandering, stopping in the various fruit/flower shops, napping and people watching in the park, and breaking for the occasional nibble or coffee. As it turns out, we should have done more nibbling and skipped dinner. Our friend Michelle was to share a cab with us and join us for dinner at a vegetarian restaurant she had heard about. While not a vegetarian herself, she was doing her best to accommodate her herbivorous friends. This was truly a case where it was the *thought* that counted. There was a wait to get into the place because it was apparently chic for the week. Once inside, the tables were so close together that servers had to suck in their non-existent guts to move around. Still, I was looking forward to the experience, expecting delicious veggie lasagna, or maybe an intense salad with some homemade bread and aged cheese. No such luck for this Chicago girl. The restaurant was not only vegetarian, but vegan as well, placing a hundred foot restraining order on all animal products. I needed help interpreting most of the menu, but they could have simplified it by categorizing the entrees into: 1.) grasses never meant for human consumption, 2.) raw vegetables cut very tiny and smashed around in decorative manners, and 3.) sauces with nothing discernible on which to place them. Oh well. The cab ride there had been so violent that an empty stomach was probably just as well.

When dinner was over, we parted ways with Michelle, concluding that the few vegetarian items offered in a carnivorous restaurant would be good enough for future dining engagements. Dinner or no dinner, this last night in New York was certainly the grand finale of the trip. Guitar legend and father of multi-track recording, Les Paul, was performing every Monday night at a small downstairs club in the theatre district. To comprehend the magnitude of this evening's entertainment, one has to understand that I grew up with a dad who played guitar and exhibited distinguished taste in guitars at that. I learned the name Les Paul along with the names Grandma, Aunt Sue, and Uncle Mike. We still sometimes refer to my dad's gold-top anniversary edition Les Paul guitar as his 'fifth child'. You get the picture.

At the time of our trip, the man was, I believe, about 83 years young. Small candlelit tables seated an intimate crowd waiting to hear Mr. Paul perform with his trio. He was sharp and witty, and sounded as good as he did fifty years ago. I am happy to report that no hubcaphones were in attendance, just straightforward guitar. His allows the tour company to double the price of an otherwise unmarketable graveyard tour. signature playful sound was intermingled with short tales and the kind of jokes that a man in his eighties has a right to tell. After the concert, the audience was invited to line up to meet Les for handshakes, pictures, autographs, or just to drool at his feet. After a pronouncement of what an honor it was to meet him, a handshake, and an autographed t-shirt for Dad, we walked a few blocks through Times Square to the subway.

Times Square is another one of those places that we were supposed to feel scared in, but did not. We encountered a few homeless people, and the normal amounts of city garbage, but at 1:00 in the morning, we witnessed no problems. We walked past several shops and theatres, including the famous Ed Sullivan Theatre, host to Elvis, the Beatles, and lately David Letterman. I suppose we could have found plenty of x-rated GIRLS! GIRLS!

GIRLS! among the flashing lights and the Jumbotron, if that is what we were looking for, but it did not seem to be an inevitable theme. Likewise, it was a quiet wait for our sub train, with just a few tired people milling about, and one or two rats running down the tracks. (Don't gape at the page like that, Reader; every city has them.) They did not bother us and we did not bother them. Besides, they probably did not even survive the next train's arrival.

We spent the next day packing to leave, revisiting our favorite streets, and doing our best to temporarily break off our affair with the city we love. When evening approached, we took a cab back to user-friendly La Guardia. We are both prompt people, and we generally arrive at the airport two hours before a domestic flight leaves. As a realist whom friends sometimes accuse of being a pessimist, I will probably always be this early. It is worth mentioning, though, that it only took about eighteen minutes to check-in, check our luggage, go through security, and find our terminal. (I told you they were efficient!) Fortunately, we had books with us, and as idle time often makes people believe they are hungry, we soon discovered the cinnamon roll vendor. These unnecessary but delicious rolls have become somewhat of a tradition as we wait in airport terminals for flights home. I guess they are sort of consolation prizes to ourselves since we know that at that point, we are only moments from ending our vacation.

In this particular case, however, moments turned into hours. Our flight was delayed due to inspection difficulties. *That's all right. Take your time. I can wait a while if it means that the plane will not suddenly fall apart over Ohio.* Eventually the flight techies determined that we would need to switch to a different plane. *Okay, but this better be legit. I've seen the Indiana Jones movies. I know all about planes ending up in countries that they're not supposed to be in, and I know exactly how long it should take to fly from New York to Chicago.* Once I was sufficiently convinced that we were headed in the proper direction (*yeah, I think I do recognize these clouds from the trip out,*) I settled into a very empty flight. In a row of six seats, the two of us could sprawl out with no one next to us, behind us, or in front of us. It was better than first class! Under these ideal flight conditions, we returned to a bright half-moon in Chicago, already planning our next New York getaway.

Chapter 3
The City That Never Sleeps: Mid-April 2004

In very little time, we became just like all the other fools who endlessly rant about the wonders of New York. Virtually overnight, we developed Woody Allenesque ramblings. After six months of trying to shield our loved ones from random outbursts of annoying New Yorkago accents, we decided we needed to venture back to the town we love. After all, there is always something new happening in the 'city that never sleeps'. As per our pattern, we worked together and then left to stay near Midway on a Thursday night. We kissed Chicago goodbye with a celebratory stuffed pizza, and then headed to our hotel.

The plan was slightly different this time. We still landed at La Guardia early Friday morning, but rather than going directly to Manhattan, we first rented a car to drive north of the city to Tarrytown. This afforded us the opportunity to visit the graveyard to end all graveyards: Sleepy Hollow Cemetery. Yes, this is a real cemetery, located a few blocks from the eighteenth century village of the same name.

If you have ever read the works of Washington Irving, or if you have ever experienced an American Halloween, you know that Sleepy Hollow was (and *is?*) the home of the infamous Hessian soldier, who, inconveniently, lacks the benefit of a head. It seems, according to the local legends that Irving himself heard as a boy that a ghost sans skull can be a very testy and jealous individual, galloping around after dark to lop off the tops of bodies that previously enjoyed their headed condition. As in all good tales, the lines of fiction and nonfiction are blurred. The church referenced in the legends lies immediately adjacent to the grounds. Furthermore, the cemetery contains the grave of Washington Irving, as well as that of a German mercenary soldier who fought in the American Revolution. Surprisingly, it is not a touristy place.

Sleepy Hollow is immense enough to earn the moniker 'city of the dead'. It is divided into sections like neighborhoods, separated by long, winding roads. Along the entire back boundary of the cemetery, roughly three blocks, runs a babbling stream surrounded by gnarly trees and shrubs, teased and tortured into twisted tenants. The residents' abodes range from simply marked graves to stone fortresses celebrating deceased money. It is easy to get lost without the map provided at the front gate, or maybe the allure of perfectly arranged hills, trees, and hedged nooks gradually draw one into this peaceful retreat. We were captured. After driving around, pausing for walks in various 'neighborhoods', we found our own niche in which to read, meditate, or contemplate Johnny Depp in the role of Ichabod Crane. Okay, that part was just me.

As the afternoon expired, we started back to the airport to return our carriage and make our way to lower Manhattan, barely early enough to outrun Friday rush-hour traffic. (We like to live on the edge.) Incidentally, Reader, now that you know that most New Yorkers do not own cars, you can understand why renting a car in the Big Apple requires a second mortgage on your home. After our economic lesson in supply and demand, we arrived at the same hotel that we stayed in last time. Due to an error in the reservation system, the hotel assigned us to a smoking room, which this wimpy traveler cannot tolerate. When we explained the problem, the management was very accommodating, giving us a lovely room on the eighteenth floor. The room had two windows: one looking out onto the street (good lighting, well-arranged view), and one looking down into the offices of some Wall Street clones (who did not a single naughty, illegal, or interesting thing the entire weekend). Once we were settled, and we confirmed that the Weather Channel was accurately describing the temperature we had experienced just moments ago, we walked to Spencer-and-Michelle's condo.

Michelle and Senator are both big Beatles fans, and Spencer seems to have a healthy appreciation for the Liverpool lads as well. While I was immediately crazy about their music the first time I heard my friend play *Hold Me Tight*, I do not have quite the same nostalgia as many other fans. In fact, many of them would shun me based on my lack of statistical knowledge alone. My defense, though, is that the Beatles arrived in the U.S. more than a decade before I arrived anywhere. Thankfully, my friends grant me a reprieve on this technicality.

Anyway, Michelle purchased tickets to a two-man play based on the events leading up to the assassination of John Lennon, as viewed through the eyes of two FBI agents sent to keep a watch on the radical. The set was very simple, designed to look like an office filing room from twenty-five years ago. One of the actors was a thin, average-looking and above-average-acting twentysomething man whose name I would tell you to remember if I could provide it. The other actor was the man who played the dad on television's *The Wonder Years*. If you do not know whom I mean, rent it when it comes out on DVD. Yes, Reader, I know I just ended my career as the World's Most Useless Theatre Critic.

Both did an excellent job. It was one of those dramas where the writing is so good that, even though you know it will end in tragedy, you are captivated by the thoughtful dialogue leading up to the climax. When the sound of a gunshot offstage informed the audience the fateful December day had come, those who did not jump in their seats jumped in their stomachs. We were left with plenty of fodder for intelligent discussion. The moral of the story: never underestimate the impact of well-exposed dreamers or well-produced off-Broadway plays.

The next day ushered us into our vow of eating only fruit in the morning, and doing plenty of walking. Why the restraint on vacation? Have we reached such a state of physical enlightenment and will power? Hardly-- it is easy to resist a large breakfast when you are going to Murray's for lunch. Having fervently studied the selection of foreign cheeses the last time we were there, one would think that it would take less time to decide on the components of our lunch this time. You should know us better than that by now. After our usual ceremonious selection, we exited the shop to find *our* bench occupied. Being the flexible tourists that we are (remember Rhode Island?), we found a park at the end of the block. If you can guard your lunch against the pigeons, it is the perfect spot for a European style picnic. Though we very rarely drink wine, I would have liked to have had an unopened bottle there as a prop... and maybe some goats roaming around...

Later that day we walked off a tiny percentage of our lunch's calories by combing the streets of Chinatown. This is not one of my favorite parts of Manhattan for two reasons: 1.) it is entirely too crowded for the small sidewalks, and 2.) every store seems exactly alike. Perhaps my taste is not discerning enough, but I really cannot tell the difference between the store on this side of the street that sells Guchi purses (*figh dolla!*), and the store on the other side of the street that sells Guccee purses (*fo dolla!*). Of course, I am being too cynical, and there are many legitimate clothing shops that sell beautiful garments. Even so, one does not have to walk too far to find beach blankets full of cheap, unreleased cds and dvds. No one seems to know why the police do not bust more illegal vendors, except that the system is so ingrained in those neighborhoods. Despite the appeals of many entrepreneurs, we did not find any treasures in Chinatown.

After a sub ride back to the financial district, we napped on large benches in the plaza by our hotel. When dinnertime rolled around, we again met Spencer and Michelle for another pioneering adventure. Tonight we would be introduced to vegetarian sushi. With more than half a year to recover from the last vegetarian experiment, we had forgotten the many abuses that can be heaped upon vegetables. Even when I used to eat seafood, I would never dream of trying real sushi, preferring the assurance that my fish would not suddenly try to swim away while inside my mouth. Without the fish, though, isn't it just rolled up vegetables, something like a cold spring roll? How could anyone mess that up?

Stupid! Stupid! Stupid! Just when I thought it was safe to expand my culinary horizons, those sneaky Japanese chefs found a loophole. It was true there was no fish in my wet little pinwheel, but I never even considered the possibility of seaweed. Curses! Foiled again! It was so fishy tasting that I could not stomach it. Clearly, the choice to go to Murray's earlier that day had been nothing short of an act of the Hand of Providence.

After multiple assurances that I was fine and our friends should not feel bad that I failed to share their sushithusiasm, our foursome taxied to another show. The comic revue *Pam An* was hosted by an outlandish and Britishly sarcastic comedian whose act attacked all of the supposed glamour of 1960s pleasure flights. Upon entering the front room of the building, we were 'searched' by security, placing purses and wallets in bins to pass down the table for inspection. When we were deemed harmless, and our tickets were deemed authentic, we were permitted to step through the circular doorway to the theatre, which was designed and decorated to look like the inside of a 747. Since our seats were 'coach', we were ushered by an overly hospitable cabin steward to the rear section, past the 'first class' passengers with their extra four inches and their champagne-filled glasses.

We were among the first ticket holders to be seated, which left us plenty of opportunity to observe our fellow audience members as they entered. It soon became apparent that this was to be a couples' event. As a matter of fact, it soon became apparent that this was to be a male couples' event. My grip on Senator tightened slightly. As the well-groomed crowd gathered, we realized that we had stumbled onto one of the hottest gay tickets in town. Don't get me wrong, the show was great; we just looked a bit conspicuous, with half of our party having boobs and all. Pam An dressed as a stewardess and shared her *real* thoughts and opinions on the passengers via voiceovers in a hilarious Ab Fab[*] way. Catering to the other 99% of the audience, though, there was a Chippendales-like dance sequence in the middle of the show with no apparent purpose. Thankfully, we were spared any nudity. My grip on Senator tightened a little more. The rest of the show featured more rapid-fire impromptu humor, and it was certainly worth the ticket price. A grand time was had by all; I am just glad no one noticed that I was wearing last year's fashion, and my hair was overdue to be dyed.

The next morning we slept in, rising late for our fruit ritual. With apples and bananas in tote, we claimed a place on the plaza outside our hotel to enjoy a lazy Sunday morning. Though neither of us are big shoppers, there is a store called Lush that we visit in Midtown Manhattan. Lush is a company that sells personal care products (shampoo, soap, and such) made of all-natural ingredients. In other words, they smash weeds, flowers, fruit, and vegetables together, and sell it to suckers like us who pay a small fortune for a bottle of Mother Nature's luxurious sweat, hence the name. Their pricey wares fall into that 'on special occasions' category of treats.

---

[*] British sit-com *Absolutely Fabulous*, featuring two fabulously tacky middle-aged shopaholic alcoholics. Watch an episode or two. Then find an AA group to join.

For all of the hype, the store is only about as big as a large garage. Friendly customer service agents/veggie-smashers wander around offering help, and often perform demonstrations of their most explosive item, the Bath Ballistic. For a cheap date, (until the conditioners entice you) go to one of their stores and watch one of the natural bath techies drop a Bath Ballistic into a pan of water. It is like a giant Alka-Seltzer for the body. Splashing, fizzing, and maybe even glitter will ensue. Shameless plug: Lush is available in the U.S., Canada, and England, and used by spoiled brats everywhere for beautiful results on their skin and hair. (Yes, I want my cut if this increases their business.)

While looking for Lush the first time, I stumbled past one clothing store that did pique my curiosity. While this would be an obvious event for many of my female friends, those who know me know that I did not receive the female shopping gene at birth. This has quite possibly been a contributing factor to a successful relationship. Simply put, I hate to shop. If I have to go to a store, I focus on the necessary object, go into the store, seize it, pay for it, and leave, rejecting all of the shopping psychology of 'impulse items'. If I can beat my old record time, so much the better.

The store that caught my attention, however, may not even have had a name for all I remember. What grabbed me was the large sloppy lettering in the window proclaiming, "Underwear, Bras $2 and Up". Now I was not naïve. I had no false expectations of uncovering Victoria's secret, or anything of real quality, but any American girl will tell you that her sub-clothing layer can cost the arm and the leg over which it slips. Even if these gems fell apart after one or two washings, it would be worth it. In I ventured. The long lines were either a sign of good deals on underwear, or just a sign of a bad economy. After perusing the selection, I found some great styles and colors. Total purchase after excruciating wait in line and semi-bilingual interchange at register: $8 for three items... and they are still in great condition. I should also mention that Senator waited outside, obviously uninfluenced by the previous evening's audience at the *Pam An* show.

We left the cheap-undies store and walked the perimeter of Macy's, where, I am disappointed to report, we saw no escaped balloons or tipsy Santas. After walking many more blocks down the Avenue of the Americas, which could more aptly be named 'Avenue of American Malls', we returned to our room to get ready for a concert. Time-Out New York magazine had alerted Senator to the fact that a small club on the East Side was hosting John Zorn's associates in an experimental jazz concert. According to the advertisement, the concert proceeds would go to benefit the Water Reclamation Act. Senator enjoys jazz and is somewhat of a John Zorn fan, and we were in the mood for something different, so we ordered tickets. After all, we are both pro-water, and the reclaiming of water sounded harmless enough, whatever it meant.

Fortunately, we arrived early enough to claim two of the few chairs available. It is not that I mind standing for concerts, but all of the water-reclaimers were sitting on the floor, and that's just not appealing in the country's most populous city. When the two musicians, (and I use the term loosely,) entered the stage, I was not quite sure what to expect, but it was not the sound that they emitted. I went with an open mind, looking forward to creative uses of sounds to produce unique forms of music. What protruded from their mess of cords, laptops, and superfluous instruments, however, was nothing more than ear-splitting screeching and the kind of grating discord that makes nails sliding down chalkboards a pleasant alternative.

I have listened to many kinds of music, most of it too loud, since I was born, but this actually hurt my ears and head. I tried to be polite, and I did not want anyone to lose their grip on their water, but I could not take it anymore. With an apologetic glance toward Senator, I got up and left. Recovering in the lobby, I halfway wondered if this was somehow going to lead to one of those miserable vacation arguments that I have witnessed other couples having. If it did, at least it would be more musical than what we had just heard. Moments later Senator joined me, confessing that he shared my opinion. It was the only time I have ever walked out of a performance, but I have the satisfaction of knowing that I made a valiant effort. It is too bad that some artists cannot tell the difference between noise and experimental music, but at least the water will not go unreclaimed.

After leaving the concert, our focus turned to food. We planned to eat dinner after the show, which did not start until 8:30pm. The late time and the chaos of the screeching had combined to make us both ravenous. Thanks to our strategic planning, we would pass right through Little Italy on the way back to our hotel. No music is so bad that great pasta cannot comfort you. We hailed a cab and instructed the driver to drop us off at pasta central. We paid him, got out, and started walking.

Hhmmm, there was nothing open in the immediate distance, but it was a beautiful night, so we walked a little further. Nothing edible stirred. We double-checked the street signs to make sure we were in New York. It was not even 10:00 yet. Isn't this supposed to be the city that never sleeps? Another mile and a half of pavement passed beneath our growling stomachs before we decided to give up. Even walking along Broadway, we found only a Dunkin' Donuts. Shifting gears from oregano to powdered sugar just would not work, though. Soon our hotel was in sight. This was unbelievable. Our only viable options were the side-by-side 24-hour delis. After pacing between the two as though one offered any better selection than the other did, we purchased cheese, tortilla chips, a banana, and a cookie, half of which were fighting for their quickly fading shelf lives. We devoured our buffet on our bed. We were slightly annoyed at the disappointment of not finding a place to eat on a Sunday night in New York City, but mainly we were just dumbfounded. Moreover, if you ever assume that you can eat a late dinner in lower Manhattan on a Sunday night, just remember that the city that never sleeps does take occasional naps.

With bellies full of junk and sheets peppered with crumbs, we drifted off to join the city in sleep. Monday morning was filled with more New York wandering, and hundreds of restaurants taunting us with their 'open' signs. After saying our goodbyes to Spencer and Michelle, and planning our next hellos with them, we hailed a cab for the airport. We easily passed through the security checkpoint at La Guardia and escorted our traditional cinnamon rolls to the terminal with us. Five months later we would return on official business, with an accordion as a traveling companion.

Chapter 4
Elvis, a Star Trek Bride, and Lots and Lots of Doughnuts: Late May 2004

Most people will agree that weddings and funerals tend to come in multiples. Fortunately, 2004 invited us to five *weddings* in the span of four months. This, in and of itself, is not so outrageous, until you realize that we were directly involved in all but one of these weddings. The season kicked off in early May, at a wedding where I was the Maid of Honor and Senator was the Musician of Honor, writing original music for the ceremony. Just two weeks later, we were to fly to Los Angeles so he could be a groomsman in a friend's wedding. Thus, we just *had* to plan another trip.

I had adapted easily enough to New York, always admiring it from afar as I grew up dreaming of its many sights and personalities. In fact, I had always fashioned myself a sort of East Coast girl at heart. Los Angeles, on the other had, fell into that category of places I definitely wanted to see... once. Of course, I wanted to go to California, mainly because it would be a new experience, and I could add one more state to my list of those visited. Likewise, Los Angeles, particularly Hollywood, held my curiosity to some degree. After all, it is Tinsel Town, and the home of glitz, motion picture magic, and plenty of stories of people 'making it'. Lucy and Ethel seemed to have a good time there. The problem was the other side of L.A. that I had heard about. I had visions of beaches that would be beautiful, if you could only see past the smog. I also pictured scores of saccharine smiles paired with other false body parts. Then there is the crime, and the earthquakes, and the mudslides, and the fires... but other than that it sounded lovely.

The only disaster I expected to encounter was the fake population, so they concerned me the most. It is one thing to deal with Barbie and Ken cruising Sunset Boulevard, knowing you can escape their disgusted gaze when the light turns green. It is a completely different matter, however, to know that you have to deal with Barbie and Ken* throughout all of the events surrounding a wedding.

The rehearsal and dinner would be Thursday. Friday would follow with a private comedy roast of the groom, a professional stand-up and television comedian. The wedding and reception would take place Saturday. While I am in fairly healthy shape, in the month of May, coming out of a Midwest winter, I am pale, a little soft, and, well, very Illinoisan. Would I be subjected to the scrutiny of judgmental plastic replicas of Frankenstein's monster, who could not get over the fact that I was not (and was not trying to be) in the 'business'? In a very short time I would have my answer, but in the meantime, my hopes of meeting any sincere characters in Los Angeles were not unrealistic.

The plan was slightly different this time. The financial realities of wedding invitations that involve plane trips helped us decide not to stay in Chicago the night before we left, as we

---

*To be clear, I am *not* referring to the bride and groom, thank goodness!

usually did. Instead, we would leave from our home early Thursday morning to go to Midway. Wednesday morning Senator left for work, and I had about two hours before I had to leave. The house was clean and the packing was basically done, so I sat down to enjoy some reading time. Then I saw it. Out of the corner of my eye, I could have sworn that I saw something dart across the floor. It couldn't be. Nothing bigger than a spider has ever invaded our domain, and each has been quickly shown the door or the end of the vacuum cleaner. I desperately hoped I was wrong; after all, they say the eyes are the first to go. Dutifully, I took a deep breath and went across the room to investigate.

    A terrified chipmunk met my gaze. Now, Reader, you must understand that I have always found rodents and their kin adorable, having rats as my first and most recent pets. This was not a matter of my fear of the animal. This was a matter of my fear of the fact that a wild animal had instantaneously become a third roommate. Along with the obvious question of how to remove him, was the greater matter of how he got in and what we would come home to find if we left town for five days as planned. After a somewhat frantic call to Senator, he advised me to purchase a humane trap and set it before going to work. After verbally enticing the creature with a description of the delicious cuisine that awaited him in the trap, and verbally threatening him if he dared to touch the books or the curtains, I left the house uneasily.

    As in every great cartoon starring small furry animals, my chipmunk snatched the bait without paying the price of imprisonment. How do they do that? I came home that night to find all of the furniture moved to the middle of the room, every light in the house lit, and my brave and adrenalized boyfriend on the warpath, broom in hand. After much strategic thinking and chipmunk psychology*, we were able to chase our unintended guest out the front door, to the mutual satisfaction of all of us. We could leave town the next day in peace.

Early the next morning, we left Chicago for Los Angeles International Airport, commonly know as LAX. I am not sure in this day and age that any airport should be known as lax, but that is another matter. I can only tell you that my first impression of the City of Angels was the smell of urine. I apologize, Reader, but the airport reeked of it. We quickly collected our baggage and headed for the taxi line. When our turn came, we were ushered to the backseat of a cab driven by a man who seemed to be the DNA recombinant of Elvis and Neil Diamond. He was very friendly, and very proud of his hometown. Correction: proud of where he *lives*; no one is born in L.A.

Elvis Diamond dropped us off at our hotel, a simple but clean establishment, complete with palm trees and located a few miles east of Hollywood. Upon settling into our room, it soon became apparent that the country's second largest city differs extremely from so many others in that you must have a car to get around. There is no subway or el train system of which to speak. Supposedly a bus line exists, but the travel guides fail to expound upon it, and locals look a bit frightened and cross themselves when the topic is brought up, not unlike the mountain people of Transylvania. We broke down and rented a car. *Yes, the economy size will be fine. Honestly, there's no one we need to impress, show up, or connect with in any way.*

Our first afternoon was unscheduled, giving us a chance to ease into California before we were confronted with 'wedding people'. We found the perfect spot for this transition at the local

---

* If ever a rodent or chipmunk enters your home, it will tend to dart quickly in a panic. It is useful to know, though, that he will generally run the same path once established. This is especially handy if he chooses to run alongside a wall, where you, the savvy homeowner, can have a trap waiting at the other end.

farmer's market. One thing I will say for California: it has the most gorgeous produce that you will ever lay eyes on. We decided that a bag of fruit, crowned by the three pounds of strawberries I felt compelled to buy, would be our breakfast for the weekend.

Even with great fruit and vegetables on hand, the subject of eating is somewhat
misrepresented by California to the rest of the country. With tanned and toned bodies, and an abundance of health food stores, one might reasonably get the impression that Californians eat well. This, like so many other impressions, fades once beneath the surface. For example, the fact that you cannot smoke in restaurants in Los Angeles seems like a health-conscious measure. The point is lost, however, when hoards of people smoke just outside the doors of every restaurant and bar. Instead of getting the smoke in wafting doses from other tables, the nonsmoker walks through the opaque barrage of concentrated nicotine before entering.

Similarly strange is the fact that it is harder to find vegetarian options in Los Angeles than it is in New York or Chicago. They exist, of course, but not to the extent that L.A.'s reputation would have you believe. In fact, what you do find on every corner are doughnut shops. From small mom-and-pop organizations to large chains, you can always find a doughnut vendor at any time of day or night. We have not quite figured out Los Angeles draw to the fried, powdered, jellied, or frosted circles of dough, but temptation is never far away. Still, you can, as the saying goes, always depend on finding plenty of fruits and nuts.

Thursday night was our first commitment to the wedding party: the rehearsal and rehearsal dinner. The wedding would take place outdoors, in a beautifully manicured garden. We arrived early to meet the rest of the party. Senator soon found out that he was one of only two non-comics among the groomsmen. Conversations centered around who had known the groom the longest, agents who were not obtaining 'good gigs', the current market for cable shows, and the new toys each had purchased. Blah blah blah.

As the men folk tended to congregate on their side, I was left to the merciless clutches of the female of the species. Actually, I am exaggerating. Everyone was friendly... a little too friendly. My introductions to the 'wives' group went something like this:

"Hi!!!! Nice to meet you!!!! Ohmigod! I *so* totally miss carbs, don't you? So how do you know (insert name of common acquaintance)? Oh, so you know him from *back home*. That's sweet! So what do you do? Real-ly, and who do you know in the industry? Well, I just happen to have some of my work if you want to take a look. My husband is currently collaborating with (insert semi-important name). Yeah, just a little thing they got going when (same semi-important loser) was up at the house last month. Well e-mail me and let me know what you think because I think we could *totally* connect on a project. I've seen some of your stuff and it is *un-buh-leev-a-bull*!!! Oops- gotta' go, agent on the cell! Ciao!"

I needed a sign that read: *I have no talent and I cannot help you so shut up and smile at me from a distance, please.* Senator, who actually does have both musical and songwriting talent, stood out by the mere fact that he did not name drop or advertise himself. This was not just characteristic of the wedding party; it happens everywhere you go. There is a very desperate and somewhat pathetic drive to promote oneself above the other million people trying to make it big. Good luck, but you can keep the pressure.

The rehearsal progressed smoothly, ushered along promptly by the first wedding coordinator I had ever met. ("Now people...") A wonderful Italian dinner followed in a second story banquet room that overlooked the sunset. We claimed our seats at the people-who-are-not-family-or-from-around-here table, next to a writer from the King of the Hill show, a very quiet couple, an extremely obnoxious girl, and her whipped-beyond-all-hope-of-healing fiancé. She made sure that we knew every detail of every trip that she had recently taken, careful to gesture in jewelry-flaunting poses. (No, Reader, it's completely different than when I give you trip details.) Thankfully, a toast by the father of the bride cut off her self-adoration.

The bride's dad, as it turns out, was one of the original members of the cast of Star Trek. Having never seen an episode of any season or version of the show, that fact meant nothing to me, but I made a mental note to look up his star on the Walk of Fame the next day. The groom, a local Chicago boy, left for L.A. many moons ago to find success as a comedian in the land of opportunity. I had met the couple the previous December when they were in the Chicago area on a holiday visit. We laughed over dinner and amazed them with tales of cheap real estate in the town to which we were moving. With the exception of a few dumb members of the entourage, it was going to be a fun wedding.

Friday morning we were again reprieved to play by ourselves. After passing dozens of competing dollar stores*, we stumbled upon the La Brea Tar Pits. Cartoons supplied the whole of my vast knowledge of the tar pits, so I was expecting something spectacular and, well, oozy. There was a small black lake near the parking lot, but it just looked like an Illinois interstate in summer, minus the orange roadwork signs. There were a few quiet bubbles coming up, but nothing dramatic or menacing. Once you looked at it for five minutes, it pretty much lost all of its wonder. Hence, we opted to skip the price of

---

*Why doesn't one of them sell junk for $.99 to corner the market?

admission to the museum of tar and tar related facts, and move on to an even greater disappointment.

This was the day I would see Hollywood. Visions of 1930s actresses with seductive eyes, swinging boas, and acceptably curvy figures, being bent over for passionate kisses from handsome actors who spoke in slow, pronounced statements, filled my mind. I pictured the entryway to Mann's Chinese Theatre, where so many red carpets had been unfurled through the ages. What kind of dress would I wear to accept an Oscar? From Groucho Marx to Harrison Ford, all of my heroes, or at least their footprints, would surround me.

I suppose I should have listened to Senator's warnings about Hollywood. He had already witnessed the distinct lack of the glamour that once made the town famous. The footprints are a unique capsule of film's history and the stars that won America's heart, but there is nothing grand about their surroundings. The theatre entrance looks like any other theatre entrance, and could just as easily be a porn palace on a side street. Forget the classy images from television and the movies. The entire block is filled with the requisite junk shops, wax museums, and fast food places that one would expect at any tourist trap.

Though I hate to admit it, nearby there was a familiar scent present as well. What is it about L.A. and the smell of urine? One walk down the famous avenue was enough. We acknowledged the father-of-the-bride star, and made our way back to our hotel.

We switched gears back to the wedding party. Tonight was a roast of the groom, provided by friends and fellow comics. In the spirit of Dean Martin and the Friar's Club, the groom was subjected to embarrassing stories about himself, and the usual insults that only close friends can hurl. His bride-to-be was warned, apologized to, and questioned on her 'insane' choice of a mate. After three hours of sidesplitting laughter between bites of dinner, the groom was released from the hot seat. Following the late, raucous night, we looked forward to sleeping in the next morning.

With just enough time to kill before we had to be back at the wedding site, we decided to take a hike on the outskirts of Burbank. One thing I can understand about people's affection for California is its topographical diversity. The ocean, the desert, the mountains, and the valleys are all within a short, albeit frustrating, drive from each other. Saturday morning called for the desert sun. Armed with enough sunscreen to repel the sun's rays all the way back to the stratosphere, I grabbed my Essential Other's hand and started an intense, uphill climb. The occasional small, loose rocks sliding were the loudest sound we heard in the course of an hour and a half. Sometimes it is amazing how quiet it can be just outside of the chaos of a metropolitan area. The exertion and dry air caught up with us a little sooner than we had hoped, but it was time to get ready for the ceremony anyway.

Just before sunset, the bride and groom met on the beautiful lawn of a fragrant, flowered courtyard, in front of the quack that posed as a reverend of some sort. I respect the desire to incorporate various religious and traditional backgrounds with modern expressions of love and devotion. This service, however, was out of control, though I think it went over very well with most of the guests. The minister/officiating body/hostess/ spiritual practitioner was a woman in her mid-fifties or so, who perfectly represented the L.A. persona. She was there to steal the show, complete with lame attempts at humor and overzealous smiles, gestures, and glances. Her flamboyance took center stage, overshadowing even the bride. To earn her pay, she impressively worked in some Christian text, a Hebrew benediction, an Irish blessing, some Native American wisdom, various Hindu and Buddhist advice, and a New Age closing. Suppressing our giggles, I from my seat and Senator from his place in the groomsmen's line, we each wondered if we were at a wedding or a United Nations conference. What ever happened to the good old days when hippies just wrote some vows to each other and forgot them halfway through the ceremony?

Nevertheless, the happy couple was hitched, and now it was time to party. Cocktails on the patio were followed by dinner in the adjacent ballroom. Guests pre-selected entrees with their R.S.V.P. cards, expediting the serving process. At this point I would like to pause to thank the bride and groom for two counts of very thoughtful planning. First, instead of some stupid keychain or flask, the groomsmen were given the tuxedo rental as their gift for participating, which was clever and highly appreciated. Second, the dates of the bridesmaids/groomsmen (including yours truly) were seated next to their significant others. I was rescued from dining alone with starry-eyed strangers. Together we could take on any city; alone, Los Angeles was just way too scary. Dancing right through to the very last song, we managed to work up an appetite.

Ever since we first planned to go to California, Senator had been promising/threatening to take me to a joint called Roscoe's Chicken & Waffles. I will give you two guesses as to what was on the menu. Fortunately, they served food until 3:00am. *Why stop then*, I thought? On the outside, Roscoe's looks like a speakeasy about to be raided, complete with bodyguard at the door. At 1:00 in the morning, there was a wait on the street to get in. The tough-looking doorman softened as he called our name. We were in... still very white, but in.

Bodies were crammed at the tiny tables in the warm dining room. It smelled like your grandma's kitchen (if you suddenly found out your grandma was from Mississippi), and since half of the two options were vegetarian, we were all set. Moments later, the most delicious, perfectly textured waffles I have ever inhaled, touched, or tasted, appeared. How chicken and waffles became paired I will probably never know, but the restaurant has a reputation for great taste and quality, and we would add our recommendations as well.

We had survived the second wedding and accompanying festivities of 2004. It was time for a lazy Sunday at the beach. As in New York, the time had come for me to meet another significant person in Senator's life. In this case, it was his sister, Carol, who lives in Mar Vista. We met up with Carol, a sweet soul who also understands hiding from the sun while enjoying it, for a walk along Venice Beach. Again, all of my prior information about Venice came from cartoons, so I entered the excursion open-minded.

In this case, the cartoons were accurate. The beach was divided among weightlifters that look like they could tip over at any time, junk vendors, entertainers, and freaks. Most are easy to pass by, or shake your head at, as with the robed, bushy-haired guitarist on rollerblades. Others deserve your attention, as with the young man who juggled dangerous objects while riding a unicycle and engaging the crowd with his quick wit. I was so impressed, that he became the first, and probably the last, street entertainer to which I ever gave money. Who knows? Maybe he is not a struggling street talent after all. Maybe he lives in Beverly Hills with a home that has closets the size of my living room.

When our walk along the beach ended, we had lunch with Carol at a local Mexican restaurant. The food was very tasty, the service casual, and the portions more aptly sized, as in New York. We then drove up to Malibu to see a college campus that overlooked perfect turquoise surf. Leaving the winding, hilly roads of the college, we went a few miles south to a boardwalk.

It was like any other tourist boardwalk, with junk vendors, food stands, a few old fishermen perched at the end of the pier, and a few dozen sea gulls hoping to intercept the fishermen's trophies. What stood out, however, was the display of over one hundred crosses crudely pounded into the sand. Apparently there had been an anti-war protest of some sort, citing casualties in Iraq. As the sun went down over the shore, the owners of the crosses began to pick them up for the night. The display was somewhat creepy, but at least it was more original than the typical election-year fare. After telling Carol good-bye and passing another twenty or so doughnut shops, we returned to our hotel for our last night in Los Angeles.

With just one day left, we had only spent time with half of the people we wanted to see. Weddings can be so time consuming, considering the vows themselves usually take only five minutes. We made plans to meet Senator's friend Kenny for breakfast. As we waited for Kenny in our booth in a beautiful outdoor garden, we noticed he was toting some extra cargo. With his wife away on business, Kenny was the sole proprietor of his baby, Sonny. For a person under two foot tall, Sonny was very agreeable, quietly amused by his surroundings. Senator, too, was enjoying his meal and conversation with his friend, yet highly aware of the presence of one of those strange little creatures called babies.

As with all parents, particularly first-time parents, the inevitable happened. "So, do you want to hold the baby?" I will give Kenny credit for being cool about it, but he is definitely a proud daddy. So back to the question. I have many years of experience working with children of all ages, and I can pretty much fake my way through such situations. Senator, on the other hand, could count on one finger his experience holding a baby, when, as he recounts, "One of those was placed on my lap once."

I was just about to jump in and rescue my man by cleverly exclaiming, in my most girly voice, "Oh, can I hold Sonny? He is a cutey-pie, isn't he?" Just as I was about throw my body between Senator and the proffered infant, he cut in by accepting the challenge. I must say, he did great, even managing a few one-handed bites while securing the tot. After an appropriate amount of time, I graciously offered to take the baby and give the boys some 'quality' time. I am not sure, but I thought I could see some sweat on Senator's forehead as he smiled a 'thank-you' toward me.

After wishing Kenny well in his business, and agreeing that Sonny was both adorable and destined for greatness, we hit a few record stores. Most of these had little to offer, but then we found Amoeba. From industrial rock to classical jazz compositions, world music to electronica, this store has everything, including records and cds. Unfortunately, the stores tended to lack the romance of Greenwich Village's small shops, but I suppose, occasionally, that the product within the store is as important as its architecture and design... occasionally.

With a full shopping bag and a smiling and dazed Senator, we drove to meet his friend Don for lunch. To appreciate the character that is Don, you have to picture him. Don is average height, slightly soft, and always wears a dramatic expression* along with his dark sunglasses. He is currently enjoying a comfortable lifestyle, finding sufficient success in the technical end of the recording business after embracing the L.A. image. At a glance, Don fits into the landscape well, driving the right car and using the right lingo, but just about the time you are ready to gag on your spoon, he opens his mouth with warm, sincere greetings. He is both gracious and polite, and he always has a moment to listen (and talk). Though we have nothing in common, save our friendship with Senator, I found Don to be an inviting host and a fresh breath from most of the city's fraudulent smiles.

In the spirit of 'keeping it real', Don gave us directions to some trails through the canyons. Following Mulholland Drive led us to ponder two items: the contrast of the rugged desert beauty with the sprawling city, and how long it would be before

---

*Early into the conversation with Don, I learned that he is a man who will get just as excited about his new high-tech office chair as a major project he is working on. I was repeatedly asked to try it out. ("Can you believe this thing? No really, sit in it! You gotta' try it for yourself!")

some of the homes slid over the side of mud cliffs. Call me crazy, but I think I might be a bit concerned if my kitchen were gradually inching out over space. I do not think the few poles placed under the corner of the house to prop it up would be enough for me. Every year people in California lose homes in mudslides, and every year their neighbors think it is just a fluke that will not happen to them. We discussed the silly cliff dwellers while hiking through some trails of low brush and cactus and observing the many species of colorful birds. This was our last L.A. adventure before preparing for our return flight.

We had a great time in Los Angeles simply because we always have fun traveling together. In and of itself, it is not a spectacular city. The people who live and work there seem to love it, but I do not care if I ever get back. I suppose it is a little more enchanting if you achieve your dreams there, but it just doesn't hold that for Senator or me. We agreed that five days was the perfect amount of time. I actually started to get a little homesick near the end, which I generally do not experience while on vacation.

Around 9:00pm Monday evening, we returned our rental car to the airport. Our flight would run overnight, landing us in Chicago around 5:30am. As I mentioned, LAX is not an endearing airport. By this time our goal was to find coffee, a cinnamon roll if we were lucky, and some seats in the terminal. To our dismay, we learned that all of the airport vendors, including Starbucks, close early. So much for our cinnamon roll tradition.

The terminal itself is a hub, housing passengers for several different gates. When they called our flight, we were supposed to line up in one area of the hub and wait to board. This turned into a cramped mess, with people tripping over carry-on bags while waiting in a sloppy line. Our flight was packed.

We were fortunate enough to have a good-natured man in the seat next to us. In fact, he was bobbing his head merrily while singing along with the ATA commercial as we waited to take off. I liked this guy. He was refreshingly, but not intrusively, oblivious to everything and everyone around him. His only concern was his one piece of carry-on luggage, his basketball. He gently cradled said companion on his lap, occasionally thumb-drumming on it to accompany his song.

That figured. One of the most down-to-earth people we saw in L.A. lived somewhere else, and was on his way home. As I clarified, we did have fun. The key is to go to Los Angeles with a sense of humor, a loved one who also possesses a sense of humor, and maybe a basketball. Moreover, if you are lucky enough to make it big there, just be sure to stay humble enough to enjoy the simple pleasures of chicken and waffles.

Chapter 5
"...And *Thank You* for Staying at the Ritz Carlton...":
Early September 2004

2004: the year of the bi-coastal weddings. After a summer of Senator rehearsing requested songs to play at Spencer and Michelle's wedding, we were on our way to the last nuptials of the season, in New York City. For his part, Senator would play keyboard and accordion to accompany his friend Tony on guitar. Their covers would provide the backdrop for the cocktail hour (or so) prior to the ceremony. Conveniently, he could use the keyboard of the band that would play the reception. Getting the accordion there, however, was our problem.

This time there were no flight delays or last-minute rodent removals; just the dilemma of how to travel with an accordion. If we checked it, there was the chance of damage. If we did not check it, there was the chance that we would not stumble into the graces of a flight attendant who would keep it up front. Buying the accordion its own seat was also out of the question, as we are not wealthy or that idiotic.

It also did not help that during our last landing in New York, we happened to witness two baggage handlers roughly tossing a guitar to each other, and then onto the conveyor belt, among which was a guitar case. You just never know who will have sympathy for an instrument. After much debate, and an hour or two of lost sleep, Senator decided that it would be all right to check it, rather than risk problems while boarding. Off we went. *Please be gentle with him. He's never flown before.*

Following a relatively smooth flight, we collected our luggage and squeezebox, and hailed the next cab downtown. We had originally intended to stay in New York four nights, but a last minute (and highly unnecessary) change in the schedule at work, bumped us back a day. As a contributing member of the festivities and his always–up-to-go-along-for-a-fun-ride girlfriend, we were treated by the bride and groom to two nights at the Ritz Carlton, near Battery Park. Friday night we would stay in our now-familiar haunt, Club Quarters, near Wall Street.

Our first mission in New York, after consulting our not-so-local forecast, was to track down some speaker wire. The groom needed extra for the sound system in the reception room. Every wedding, regardless of how careful the planning, has those last minute snafus that require someone to do some busy work. The someones in these cases have to be involved with the wedding enough not to mind running around on short notice, but not so involved that they cannot spare an extra hour during the crucial weekend. Enter us.

During our past New York excursions, we had spent plenty of time leisurely wandering up and down Broadway. Now it was time to test our memory. We both recalled seeing a Radio Shack somewhere along those travels; it was just a question of where. We had checked a phone book, but we had problems finding a listing for one on Broadway. There was nothing to do but start hiking, keeping our city-scout eyes peeled for the familiar red logo. A few blocks into the quest, Senator vaguely remembered that he might have seen the store on one of the side streets. The first one yielded no rewards, but the second street, still only a ten-minute walk from our hotel, held the grand prize.

With more than enough speaker wire to support ten receptions, we returned to our hotel to await further instructions. Shortly thereafter, Michelle called, inviting us over to meet the fam. We walked the short distance to her home, and rode the elevator up four floors. Upon entering, we were greeted by the bark of their two big dogs, which need reintroductions every time we see them. Once this is established, they usually spend the rest of the weekend 'guarding' us and running around as if we are all long lost pals. After hugs to Michelle and pats to the dogs, we met her mom, sisters, and a brother-in-law. If I were any good with names, I would give them all their props here. I am definitely not good with names, however, so suffice it to say that they were a very welcoming and carefree bunch, ready to get down to the serious business of wedding weekend partying.

As kind as they all were, inviting us to join them for lunch, we felt it would be best to let the bride spend some time alone with her family. Okay, the truth is, this would be the only day we could make our escape to Murray's. As you will remember, Murray's is the world's greatest cheese shop, located in Greenwich Village. To prolong the anticipation, we walked to Murray's, and then stopped in the music store a few doors down. What could be better than the knowing that wonderful cheese and pesto are only moments away? Answer: finding a heretofore-unpossessed Kraftwerk bootleg while knowing that cheese and pesto are only moments away!

Senator turned me on to the 1980's style krautrock/electronica band early on in our relationship, serenading me with such love songs as *Tour de France* and *The Man-Machine*. It was worth the walk just to witness his delight at finding another of their unreleased concert gems. This was going to be a good weekend. He paid for his purchase, and we continued out into the street, driven by the lure of fromaggio.

After the requisite twenty minute decision period, we selected the components of our lunch, (something old, something new, something Italian, nothing bleu,) and found a spot in the park. Planning the weekend's flow of events would give us an excuse to sit for a while as the food digested. Friday was our only 'free' night, so we would find a small concert somewhere, and maybe try to meet up with another friend (also named Tony) who had flown in for the wedding. Scoping the available entertainment, we learned that Bill Frissell and Joe Lovano were going to perform that night. It sounded like a relaxing way to spend the evening before a busy weekend, so we began the walk back to the hotel to get ready.

Following plenty of time to get dressed and pass a quiet hour reading in the plaza with toned down city sounds in the background, we found a sub that could take us up to Chelsea for our concert. The performance was in a small downstairs venue with a staircase that could not possibly be wide enough to satisfy fire codes. Nobody could see the beginning of the line, or the box office, as both were buried downstairs beneath the sea of people. Senator squeezed his way between the line and the wall until he could talk to someone who worked there. Yes, there were still tickets, but they only accepted cash. Since we did not foresee the problem of a legitimate establishment in New York that would not take major credit cards[*], we could not buy tickets. Lame.

Just as we were standing on the sidewalk, looking stupid and trying to decide what to do next, we saw a familiar face approaching. Tony came to join us at the concert. He, too, was cashless, or at least he did not have enough with him to cover

---

[*] Just as in the case of not being able to find and open restaurant on a Sunday night, the largest city in the U.S. still has a very small-town feel in some places. Lesson: always bring extra cash and munchies.

three plastic-toting tourists. There was nothing else that we cared to do in that neighborhood, and it was a balmy night, so we found a café with an outdoor patio and ordered appetizers. This gave us time to socialize, catch up, and make fun of the occasional freaks that passed by. I'm sure the concert would have been fun, but sometimes it is better just to soak in the general atmosphere casually, than to be corralled with a specific group of people in a tiny, stale basement. When the polite server at the restaurant ran out of ways to drop hints that they were closing, we paid (by credit card) and parted ways with Tony. Back at the hotel, we spent a few calm moments together looking at the skyline before falling asleep. Tomorrow the wedding chaos would begin.

Saturday was packed with activity. We started the day by 'moving'. As I mentioned, Spencer and Michelle booked us a room at the Ritz Carlton for Saturday and Sunday, so we grabbed a cab to take our gear and us (c'mon little accordion) to Battery Park. The hotel perched itself at the very tip of Manhattan, with views of Lady Liberty and Ellis Island. As our cab stopped at the front door, Senator went around to the trunk to get the bags as I paid the fare, as was our established routine. (We were quite streamlined by this point.)

His efforts were soon interrupted by the doorman of the hotel, who all but knocked him over to beat him to getting our luggage out. Okay, so that's how that works. We thanked and tipped the eager icon of hospitality. Once inside, it was more of the same. There were people stationed in the lobby, who, as far as we could tell, had the sole purpose of standing, hands folded behind them, and saying in their most funereal voices, "Thank you for staying at the Ritz Carlton." *Hey, no problem, pal.*

Due to a minor mix-up at the front desk that was resolved easily enough, we were special targets of the swarthy greeting anytime we ventured toward the front entrance. To tell you the truth, it got rather annoying after the first five times. We considered making a mad dash from the elevator to the door, just to see if they would say it any faster, or with any more intensity, but we decided against it. After all, we were guests. Still, it was tempting to try to initiate a Marx Brothersesque scene.

When we found our room, several stories up, we immediately set our things down to explore. The bedroom was spacious and luxuriously austere, complete with a grand armoire that contained the mini-bar, should you get a taste for a three dollar lunch-sized bag of chips. The gracious room service menu lay suggestively nearby on the table. We viewed the large bed, and I wondered if the comforter was squishy enough to drown me in its massive puffiness. Next to the bed, we spotted the cd player. In went the new Kraftwerk find, and there it stayed until we checked out. All of this encapsulated our expectations, but then we saw the bathroom.

The crown jewel was about the size of our bedroom at home, only lined in marble. The glassed-in shower and oversized bathtub were roomy enough to easily make them the focus of a vacation. As is the case with many large bathrooms, there was a separate toilet room. As is not generally the case with toilet rooms, however, there was a telephone in the toilet room. I assumed this was for the rushed business traveler who was forever improving on his multitasking skills.

Soon after settling in, our phone rang. It was Tony and his wife Pam. Senator and Tony would play music before and during the ceremony the next day, but in the meantime, we were the default tour guides for the couple. Like two wide-eyed kids, they followed our lead to the nearest subway station, where we picked up a train to the Central Park area. Both Tony and Pam were eager to see the home of the late John Lennon, and as you now know, I am always up for a historical site, so we went respectfully (almost oddly so) past the house, and into the park.

Several feet in from this west side entrance, there is a mosaic in the sidewalk dedicated to the memory of John Lennon. Appropriately, it is entitled, 'Imagine'. Faithful devotees of the late Beatle keep the display filled with fresh flower petals. I am more of a fan than a disciple, but it was visually appealing, nonetheless. After a brief walk through the park on a picture-perfect day-- and we had even forgotten to check the Weather Channel-- we left to get a small bite to eat and catch our sub back to the hotel.

The festivities kicked off a few hours later with the arrival of the party van. Most run-of-the-mill rehearsals assign everyone to meet at a church, where they listen to a minister preach the role of each person, where he or she should stand, how he or she should walk, and when he or she should take the flowers, present the ring, etc. etc., followed by a pasta/roast beef/fried chicken dinner at a restaurant that has good group rates. Not so with this wedding rehearsal. In typical Spencer and Michelle carefree style, the 'rehearsal' consisted of the statement that, "Everyone pretty much knows what they're supposed to do. It's no big deal."

The hired van picked up the wedding party and family members at several different hotels, where, with drinks in hand, everyone rode to a restaurant just north of town. Spencer and some of his friends, who were also chefs, had prepared a large gourmet buffet of unusual dishes. The group converged on the small, candlelit bistro to enjoy food, conversation, food, wine, food, and lots of laughs. I don't recall much being said regarding any technical plans for the wedding day. We just knew that it would take place in an old photography studio, with the ceremony inside, and the hors d'oeuvres and reception on the roof. The Jewish-Lithuanian ceremony would be a tapestry of traditional and modern threads, with the guests sufficiently lubricated not to notice any minor flaws.

When the food was demolished and the pile of empty wine bottles grown, the party was safely delivered to their various hotels. With everyone too wired to go to bed, and with the knowledge that wise forethought had planned an evening wedding, several of us decided to get together in the lounge of the Ritz *("Thank you for staying...")*. The small, yet distinguished room overlooked the Statue of Liberty and the handful of boats that were meandering around in the bay. Beautiful by day, it was even more impressive at night.

Our giggly bunch only included seven people, but we sounded more like a troupe of twenty. While the drinks certainly enhanced the amusement, the main fodder for the conversation's sport was Senator's appreciation for Kraftwerk. In a moment of hysterical brilliance, Michelle and I determined that, should Daver ever start playing German electronica, we would be his backup robots. When the bar was closing and we were almost hoarse with laughter, we parted ways to get some sleep.

The next morning, late morning, that is, was sunny and relaxed. Unlike some of our companions from the previous night, we did not set ourselves up for hangovers. Instead, we felt well rested and hungry. We knew it would be several hours before we ate, so we contemplated our options. The room service menu still lay on the table. Hhmmm. Well, it wasn't as if anyone would be thanking us for staying at the Ritz Carlton again anytime soon, so we went for it. Looking over the menu, we learned that vegetarian choices were slim. (Apparently, vegetarians fall into a demographically lower income bracket than the hotel's typical guest.) We selected, of all things, pizza. Now before you judge us as hopeless white trash, Reader, understand this: when the pizza arrived, it was a gourmet pie with loads of fresh, delicious vegetables, a blend of imported cheeses, and an immaculate presentation. The fact that the server came in, set up our table, complete with tablecloth and silver settings, and pushed in each of our chairs, added to the effect as well.

With five-star pizza satisfying our tummies, we left for the wedding site. Upon arriving, we found an organized flurry of activity. With a good-luck-see-you-on-the-flip-side-Baby kiss, Senator unloaded the accordion and his recording equipment, and I left to help with tablecloths and centerpieces. Shortly into the process of lighting the first candle, I heard a very dismayed Senator. "Oh, no!" Despite our prayers, the accordion did not survive the plane trip completely. The button panel was pushed in. We immediately surrounded it for instrument surgery. Screwdriver? Screwdriver. Not small enough. What about the one on my key ring? Still too big. (I mop the sweat from Senator's forehead.) Credit card? Fingernail? After a rough job, it was in playable condition, if not perfect.

When everything settled down, just before the guests began to arrive, Senator and Tony started their set. It went very well (better than either had expected), and the bride and groom were pleased. About an hour and a half later, everyone went downstairs for the ceremony. The rabbi performed a serene, yet humorous ceremony, keeping the jolly guests involved. The only interruption in the natural and unrehearsed flow was the obnoxious solo of a girl who, though possessing a sonorous voice, had no concept of time. This can be a good thing in appropriate settings, such as lazy days on beaches, or while reading a good book, but it does not work so well when singing. Senator played faster to keep up with her. The he slowed down to meet her pace. Then he stopped and restarted time through planetary retrograde calculations. Nothing helped. Absorbed in herself, she had no clue. Mercifully, the song was not too long, and she was situated off to the side, leaving the audience to focus on the bride and groom.

Immediately following the ceremony, guests were ushered to the next room for a buffet style dinner, also prepared by the chef posse. The final stage of the wedding took place back on the roof. The reception kicked off to the cover tunes of the Chicago area band, Mr. Blotto. The temperature had dropped somewhat, and it even seemed a little drizzly at times, but it was hard to resist dancing with the moon and the Empire State Building as the backdrop. We had fun, as we always do on a dance floor (or dance roof), but most importantly, the bride and groom achieved the unique wedding that they had labored so hard to coordinate.

In keeping with this unusual approach to a usual event, the bride and groom did not leave right away for a honeymoon. Instead, the next morning they hosted a brunch in their suite at the hotel. High above Battery Park we nibbled bagels, fruit, and cheese, and enjoyed a well-earned cup of coffee. We gave our congratulations and best wishes to the bride and groom, and smiled at each other, secretly glad to be done with weddings for the year. We had survived them all, and had fun in the process. Now it was time for us to just be tourists.

Somehow I managed to go a few decades as a history lover without going to Ellis Island. Now I would finally get my chance. Since September 11, 2001, security measures have obviously increased, to the point where the checkpoint to get on the ferry is as extensive as it is to get on a plane. We had to pass through metal detectors and have our backpack x-rayed. As a person who is generally untrusting anyway, security checks never bother me, but a few people seemed irritated.

When we arrived on the island, the building, with its famous large, arched windows, looked just as it does in the century-old photos. The entrance spills open to a great hall, where you can imagine the mobs of bodies awaiting acceptance into the New World. We walked the side rooms, where doctors and psychologists inspected each individual, labeling him or her with coded letters if a problem was detected.

Next to these rooms were displays of recovered personal belongings, and writings from the few immigrants who knew English. Many spoke of their simultaneous hopes and fears, and their plans for finding relatives who preceded them to New York. We then found the kiosk of registered names. Not surprisingly, nothing came up under 'Valkovich'; my family has never had luck finding any others in the United States. 'Zuchowski', on the other hand, yielded a direct ancestor of

Senator's. With this historical heritage souvenir, we boarded the ferry back across the harbor.

There was just enough time to walk back up to the financial district and grab lunch before making our way to the airport. We spotted a crowded and loud (two good signs in New York) deli, and ordered a couple of sandwiches to go. To enjoy the last of our sunny New York afternoon, we ate outside, in a sunken plaza. For such a large city, we are always able to find a suitable picnic spot. When lunch was finished, we picked up our baggage and took a cab to La Guardia.

By now the process was routine. We made our easy trip through registration and security, ordered our ritualistic cinnamon rolls and coffee, and parked our bottoms in the terminal. Everything pointed to a smooth flight and an easy trip home. This is probably the part where you think that I am about to transition to some cataclysmic event that changed everything, the calm before the storm.

It isn't. It was later that week that we expected things to get hectic. Due to more work scheduling changes (again, highly unnecessary,) we were leaving for our longest vacation to date in just five days. Until then, we were satisfied to sit back and enjoy the ride.

Chapter 6
Badlands, Good Rolls, and Some Really, Really, Big Heads: Mid-September 2004

Few things beckon to one like beautiful and expansive scenery. Few things, that is, except maybe a perfect cup of coffee with a slice of tiramisu while reading a great book... or the employment of a flawlessly witty retort... or dancing uninhibited to your favorite song... or a moonlit tryst in an empty forest... Okay, apparently many things equally ensnarl my senses. Nonetheless, it was time for our first true road trip. The target of our motoring and camping ambitions was the great American West. After so many trips east, we would now indulge Senator's passion for large stretches of nothingness. Hence, we would roam where the buffalo had homes, and frolic among the playing deer and antelope, while making white-man reparations to the natives via tourism dollars.

Several months before our trip I had purchased a truck, lovingly dubbed 'Trucky', which I assumed would be our carriage to the west. In a rare proclamation by the benevolent

King of the Castle, however, I was informed that we would rent a car instead of putting miles on Trucky. All right. After doing my best to convince Trucky not to take it personally, Senator arranged the rental of a Chevy Malibu. *Maybe I'll look like Barbie while driving it.*

With just a few days' rest from our last excursion, we drove fifteen miles east to rent the car to drive west. Things went smoothly until we got home and, noticed, thankfully, that the answering machine had fielded a call during the brief time we were gone. *Hello, David and Wendy. This is Scott from Enterprise Rent-a-Car. I have your driver's licenses here. You probably want to come get them... unless you're already gone... hope not. Okay, bye.* Go ahead: ask if either one of us has ever left our driver's license anywhere before. With a few mutters about lost time, we packed the car, drove back east to pick up the crucial mug shots, and headed west, take two.

Soon enough, (meaning once we left Illinois,) the drive became quite pleasant, winding along gently into the rolling hills of Iowa. There was nothing to do now but follow the road and pick up *The Fountainhead* again. A somewhat sporadic and quirky aspect of our relationship is the on-again-off-again two-person book group we attend, as of yet unnamed. Despite its irregular meetings, we are proud to report that we have maintained our 100% attendance rating. The group's most recent choice was philosopher-novelist Ayn Rand's *The Fountainhead*. Senator brought this book to the group's attention, supporting the nomination with fond memories of reading it some twenty years ago and being moved by it. For those of you who have never read this lovely tome, I will sum up its 742 pages:

Howard Roark was a bratty redhead architect who hated everything that might vaguely be called 'traditional'. This was his way of rebelling against The Man of early-Twentieth Century New York. The more famous/infamous he became, the crabbier he got. The more people desired his buildings, the more he liked to existentially tell them where they could shove their Corinthian columns.

In between brooding, he finds time to pursue and be pursued by, and reject and be rejected by, and pretend he doesn't care about and re-pursue the stunning vixen, whose name currently escapes me. Everything that happens only happens because he means for it to happen. After 700 pages of proving how avant-garde he is, he falls victim to one of literature's most miserably cliché endings. With this in mind you can understand why the book, which we began two weeks prior to the trip, still needed thousands of miles for completion.

Reading on, we crossed into Minnesota. Under a vibrant pink and red sunset, we pulled into a KOA for our first night of kamping. All we needed was a short night's rest and a shower, and we would be Dakota-bound in the morning. The tent came together easily, but as I stepped back to look at it, something was horribly awry. Though we had used the tent a year earlier without incident, neither of us noticed when packing that we had left out the all too kritical rain fly.

Krap! Go ahead: ask if either of us has ever forgotten a major portion of sleeping accommodations before. In all fairness, I am reasonably sure it was my fault that it was left home, but that did nothing to stem the flow of unenlightened words that filled my head, which I aimed at no one in particular. We did not even have a tarp to tie over it hillbilly fashion. By this time, the sun was quickly abandoning us to our dilemma. We trudged back to the kamping office and upgraded our tent site to a kabin.

Trying to convince ourselves that a rough start probably signified a smooth finish in some theory of the universe, we kept a positive attitude as we awoke with sore backs and an ambitious cold navigating its way through Senator's ears, nose, and throat. A few hours later, we exited Interstate 90 to join the tens of thousands of tourists in the world who can say they have been to the Corn Palace of Mitchell, South Dakota. The convention center sported half-completed murals, decorated in various hued corncobs.

Given the time of year, it was really more of a Leftover Corn Husk Palace, but what do you want for free? Besides experiencing the wonders of vegetable art, it was here that we first realized that, while it was true that we avoided the kid season by traveling in September, we arrived in the immediate epicenter of the senior travel season. Busloads of America's fastest growing demographic group would tail us throughout the trip, snapping pictures in the road with no regard to rapidly approaching traffic. Behold, our future...

Continuing west, gauged by the increasing presence of Wall Drug billboards, the scenery became more and more rugged, finally landing us in the heart of the Badlands. While I romanticize dense forests and babbling streams, Senator pines for vast, barren landscapes of desolation, which I secretly attribute to the effective songwriter's need for small but consistent doses of despair. Surprisingly, he had never been to the Badlands, and what I remembered about their ever-changing colors and shapes drew me back eagerly. After checking into our cabin, and kicking myself again for the conspicuously absent rain fly, we drove out to a remote trail for a picnic lunch, a brief chipmunk-teasing interlude, and a short hike.

Every part of the day brings a new look to the Badlands. We arrived at noon, which is the perfect time if you like gradually emerging drama. At midday, you cannot see a whole lot of depth in the rocky spires. They appear a moonlike white, and the sky is bright blue. In the late afternoon, the sky slides from the blue scale into the pink, bringing deeper angles and a sandy coral hue to the landscape. By dinnertime, the hills are on fire. Oranges, reds, and almost menacing shadows reveal every hidden twist and crag. Slowly the night washes away the color, and the moon and stars steal the stage. The next morning wakes up purple, fading hour by hour to once again become the placid noon façade.

The second day in the Badlands began, of course, with a hike. At an altitude of about seventy-five feet above our starting point, it started to rain. Besides getting wet, the one thing you must do when a brief downpour hits the rock is take your time. It is amazing how slippery a trail becomes in just a few short minutes. Steps that you subconsciously depended on for the return trip down vanish and rearrange themselves. Yes, to all the moms reading this, we realize that we probably never should have gone in the first place. Even so, we found our footing and placed our dripping but intact selves into the car to drive to the nearby Pine Ridge Indian Reservation.

Most reservations have a poverty rate over 90%, and Pine Ridge is no exception. Abandoned cars hold a decade's worth of weeds, and random undernourished children and dogs dot the shanty scene. Though it has been more than a century since the natives were first stripped of their dignity and corralled, any pride in one's Caucasian heritage quickly melts against this background.

Nowhere was this eerie feeling of a confused and detached apology more noticeable than at Wounded Knee. We toured the small visitor's center, attended by a silent Pine Ridge resident. The museum told the history of the massacre of Wounded Knee, and various other invasions by the United States. Flags, photographs, weapons, and newspaper clippings constructed the heavy atmosphere. The only break in the solemnity was a poster with a few ancient warriors standing firm, with primitive artillery ready. The caption beneath them read: Defending homeland security since 1492.

Upon exiting the museum, we walked the windy 150 yards or so to the graveyard. As I have explained earlier, graveyards tend to find their way into most of our excursions, and as a social historian, I revel in each one. Though I am eternally grateful for the experience, I cannot call Wounded Knee 'enjoyable'. In the space of a few moments, the sky became a very dark slate color, and the wind whipped the many plastic and shabby homemade memorial trinkets about the headstones. We are not superstitious, but I will say, (and Senator will attest to this fact, as well,) that there was what I would call a very oppressive aura surrounding this area.

A few tourists stood photographing the monument dedicated to those who fell while defending their homes in the battle. A few more meandered around the other plots, trying to translate the meaning of the scene, then and now. As we left, one of the reservation's inhabitants approached us with a rehearsed plea for money. This is a common occurrence on any reservation that contains a 'tourist stop'. When we got back inside the car, it began to rain again. The ride to the cabin was quiet and introspective, maybe out of sincerity, maybe as a couple of white kids on vacation, feebly attempting to be conscious of human rights.

As the day progressed with intermittent showers, we decided to forgo the trusty camp stove and dine in the locally run café. Somewhere in Iowa, I had acquired a craving for a cinnamon roll, which I patiently planned to consume at Wall Drug during the next day's requisite stop. For tonight, though, I needed something to appease the sweet tooth. On the menu I discovered a sugarfied concoction called 'fry bread'.

Curious, I asked the server one of the world's stupidest and most common questions. "Is this good?" (As if she was going to tell me that it tasted terrible and the last four people to order it were never heard from again.) *Hhmmm, that was a pretty convincing 'yeah' that she gave me.* We ordered the fry bread and delved into the piece of heaven. Fry bread would be the Native American answer to funnel cake... if funnel cake was very good and prepared by your mom instead a toothless carnie. We savored the puffy cinnamon and sugar dessert, assuring ourselves that calories and fat were the white man's creations, and therefore, do not count if eaten on a reservation.

Day four of our longest trip together thus far began with another morning hike, despite Senator's stubborn head cold. No, we had not learned our lesson about hiking under potentially rainy skies, but the weather cooperated while we climbed and descended. It was Mount Rushmore day. En route to Keystone, however, the ancient religion of the Dakotas states that all tourists must, at least once in their lifetime, make a pilgrimage to Wall Drug. If you have not yet had the pleasure, Wall Drug, which began humbly enough, has, since the 1930s, exploded into a kitschy strip mall of 'western' gifts, junk food, convenience items, books, pricey Americana, and all the free ice water you can drink. It is fun to walk through, and legitimate history lines the wall in the form of sepia photographs, but I held no false pretense. I was here for the cinnamon roll.

Wandering through the world's largest drug store, I could almost feel the sweet frosting dripping down my throat. Finally, we came to the bakery. *Muffins, lovely. Doughnuts, very nice. Croissants, good presentation. Now for the cinnamon rolls... which are...where? Ooh, I guess I get fresh ones out of the oven.* (Casually) "Senator, do you see the cinnamon rolls anywhere?" He could not find the gems, either. *This is not funny. Where's my stinkin' cinnamon roll? I've waited through four states for this!* It soon became apparent that I was getting no cinnamon roll, world's largest drugstore or not. Unbelievable. With so much build-up for the nonexistent pastry, nothing else looked good. I sulked over my black coffee while Senator ate breakfast.

Shaking the dust of Wall Drug from my feet and vowing never to return, I took my place in the car, and we headed for the heads. Howard Roark was still moody, too. We entered the flowing tree-carpeted land of the Black Hills. As we neared Keystone and Mount Rushmore, something made me perk up. "Senator! Stop! I mean, not here, but we have to turn around!" My patient companion, wondering, but knowing me well enough not to question or think it through too hard, pulled into a parking lot to turn around. I had seen a banner, which may or may not have been illuminated by angelic light. (I am still not sure to this day.) It read, in huge letters across the entire roof of a cafe: GIANT CINNAMON ROLLS! This confirmed what I had always believed. 1.)There is a God; and 2.)He created cinnamon rolls. *Ha! In your face, Wall Drug!* Not only were said rolls giant, as advertised, but they were the most delicious cinnamon rolls I have ever tasted.

With my belly full and my petty vindication achieved, we drove to Mount Rushmore. What can I say about this internationally recognized symbol of freedom, strength, artistry, ingenuity, etc.? There are four really big heads. They are even bigger than they look in *North by Northwest*. You could take a nap in Lincoln's nostril, provided you had a means of illegally climbing into it, supporting yourself vertically once there, and a desire to do so. Amazingly, no one was killed during the construction of the monument; however, apparently many people have had brushes with danger since then, as there are guardrails everywhere. We linked arms and made our way through the Golden Pass-ers in the visitor center, and out the door to view the decorpusated presidents.

During our quest to find non-tent accommodations in the Black Hills, we came upon some cottages set among small hills and rocks, with homey stone paths connecting them. It looked like it might be expensive, but there was still vacancy, and girls who forget rain flies can't be choosey. The owners seemed genuinely pleased to see us, which concerned my skeptical mind a bit. When we saw the room, though, all fears were alleviated. It was a log cabin suite with a large t.v., clean bathroom, and plenty of space. On top of that, it was very affordable, and just a mile from Custer State Park, the next day's destination. I have often wondered why places like this get passed up, especially when crummy hotels are filled to capacity. However and whyever, I am glad we found it.

Wednesday was another full day, commencing with a call to Teacher Dave. Two explanations are necessary to understand this statement: 1.)Senator and I are the last two people in America who do not have cell phones, meaning that the rare pay phone call costs roughly the same amount as a flock of messenger pigeons; and 2.)Teacher Dave is a friend who, coincidentally, is a teacher named Dave, who moved to South Dakota about a month before our trip. We set a dinner rendezvous with Teacher Dave and drove into Custer State Park, home of hundreds (thousands?) of repopulating buffalo. Wild goats, mules, deer, prairie dogs, and others also call the park home. After pausing for the goats' right-of-way, and the lumbering buffaloes' photo shoot, we circled the park and stopped to cook breakfast. Perhaps one day we will develop the vegetarian's guide to camp cooking, with such treats as eggs n' soysage with veggie shreds, or the ultimate grilled cheese sandwich.

Checking progress in *The Fountainhead*, we drove west toward Jewel Cave. One or two of Howard Roark's buildings sold, and he continued to detest the men that bought them. Jewel Cave is supposedly one of the better examples of the different types of mineral formations. The variety of colors and textures lived up to their acclaim, and it is one of the few tours that take you several stories up and down into the cave, as well as through tight spaces and very large 'rooms'. I have been to several caves, and this was my favorite. If you go there, wear comfortable shoes. There are over 700 stairs on this tour!

When our spelunking adventure ended, we headed north to Spearfish, through miles of national forest and past dozens of waterfalls. Reaching the small college town, we met Teacher Dave at a hip little bistro, where we ordered a few messy little veggie dishes and some homemade bread. Everything seemed diced and chopped to bits, but it was very fresh and tasty. Perhaps the chef just received a new food processor, as seen on t.v. Our host entertained us with stories of the laid-back attitude of his new hometown. As we all grew up near Chicago, where things are distinctly *not* laid-back, we told him to hurry up and get to the next story.

We said our good-byes and good-lucks to Teacher Dave, and drove into Wyoming. Wyoming is prime cowboy country, and this is only one of the many reasons I have never cared for it. Nevertheless, I had not been there in many years, so I was prepared to explore it with a fresh enthusiasm. After all, I had never seen Yellowstone, so maybe this would change my perception of the big, dusty, square plain of a state. We found a quiet motel and settled in with a low budget cable movie and a box of tissue for Senator's runny nose.

The vacation goals for Wyoming were threefold: Devil's Tower, Yellowstone National Park, and Grand Teton National Park. Devil's Tower is not quite as ominous as the name suggests, as long as you do not make the mistake some others have, and attempt to free climb it. The large land mass rises hundreds of feet out of an otherwise flat landscape, with long, vertical, rail-like rock formations along the sides. Legend has it that a great bear was chasing some children who prayed for protection. In response to their appeal for help, the earth grew up underneath them, raising them to safety. The bear's claws are responsible for the long scrape marks. Perhaps most important, it is easily accessible to hikers, families, and, yes, seniors. An easy walk around the spruce-surrounded base gives a 360-degree view of all the crevices, and the occasional rock climber. It is worth going to see, as long as you are not planning to do anything else that day, due to its extreme isolation. We spent the remainder of our day driving across the state to Yellowstone.

The plan was simple enough. We would arrive at Yellowstone in the early evening, secure a place to sleep, cook a fine propane dinner, and maybe even attend a ranger guided evening program that would expose us to the wonders and mystique of the nation's first national park. The first component of this occurred. We arrived at Yellowstone around 6:00pm, which was exactly the time when the only road into the park within a five-hour radius closed for construction. Of course, no one could tell us how long it would be impassable. We decided to drive the few miles back and forth before the entrance to look for a room. Naturally, everything was full, outrageously expensive, or run by three guys getting drunk on their porch and eying us up and down as we got out of our car.

Rumor had it that the road would be open in a few hours, maybe. We had no choice but to sit, wait, and remind ourselves that this was all part of the adventure. Around 7:30pm, the road opened, but we were warned to expect more delays. Why someone thought it would be a good idea to start construction in the middle of one of the country's most popular parks, during the tourist season, in the evening, with the closest detour road sixty miles out of the way, is beyond me. Driving to the next closest entrance took over two hours.

To kill time and remain sane, I read from the park newsletter by flashlight. Schedules of ranger programs we missed, explanations of the thousands of fire damaged acres, and bear warnings took up most of the paper. Did you know that you are not even supposed to wear deodorant when camping in 'bear country'? I could see the headlines: Two Mauled in Grizzly Attack—Rangers Blame Speedstick. I guess having clean-scented armpits was one benefit of not being able to camp.

Around 10:00pm, we found a room in West Yellowstone, Montana. Something about crossing the state line made it feel even longer, but at least we were not sleeping in Wyoming. We agreed to regroup and re-enter the park in the morning. I did an abbreviated version of the Weather Channel dance and we retired.

As a good night's rest will often do, ours refreshed us, and we were even anticipating wandering Yellowstone's famous terrain. It helped that our room, which was one of the few vacancies in town, was a large and comfortable suite. On our way to check out, I noticed on the back of the door that the regular price of the room was supposedly $400.00 per night. (We had not paid a quarter of that.) Things were looking brighter.

With the sun climbing through the pines, we drove through the west entrance to the park, back into Wyoming. While Poe and a succession of literary critics would debate me, I chose to view the great black ravens that dotted the scenic pull-offs as benevolent symbols. Living so close to the wildest life of them all, the Tourist, these magnificent birds were practically tame. *Do you suppose we could bring...* "No, Wendy. I'm sure that's illegal or something. Maybe you could find some other pet to name Annabel Lee." With our feathered friends observing our every move, we walked the paths between steamy geysers and geothermal pools. The billowing steam met the chilly morning air in a burst of rainbow mist. The rocks and minerals give some of the baths a brilliant turquoise color, marred only by their omnipresent smell of sulfur.

We moved on to the gurgling mud pots. These chocolate pudding ponds bubble, blurp, and live up to their cartoon reputations. Never has boiling dirt looked so inviting. In fact, the only thing grander was Old Faithful itself. This predictable geyser performs its duty every hour-ish, earning a significant portion of Wyoming's tourism dollars. The mystery lies not in when or whether OF will erupt, but how. Sometimes a small spray disappoints crowds; other times a volcanic torrent of water rockets several stories into the air. We witnessed the latter variety. I told you the ravens were lucky.

Having exhausted Yellowstone in half of a day, we were more than happy to proceed to the Grand Tetons to the south. A French explorer with an appreciation for the female form named this triple-peaked range. Les Grands Tetons, or, The Big Breasts, soar above lush meadows and pristine lakes. This park is western Wyoming's Cinderella. Yellowstone gets all of the publicity, (and, consequently, the crowds,) while the Grand Tetons quietly display their unsurpassed simplistic beauty, with far less acclaim.

Energized by Yellowstone's superior stepsister, we chose a campsite. Though we were still rain flyless, we purchased a generic tarp somewhere in South Dakota that would sufficiently see us through the clear night. After securing our home, cooking lunch, and destroying all evidence of food to dissuade snacking bears, we drove to a trailhead. The path was only two or three miles, but it climbed up and down, and wound its way through various vegetation, so it would be a moderate challenge. We rounded a foothill, crossed a heavily flowered valley, and climbed to the top of another hill. An aquamarine lake situated at the top rewarded our efforts. One could easily lose track of a day by lying on one of the boulders at the lake's edge, in view of the Tetons.

We coaxed ourselves away in order to finish our hike before dinnertime. Passing through a miniature forest of white, gnarly trees, we came to a rushing stream. Senator had been faithfully documenting the hike via camera, executing several calendar-worthy shots. With a timed delay on the shutter, we constantly sped through our routine: pose Wendy, check frame, run/dive/jump into pose, and smile together casually, just before it snaps the picture. Locating a prime spot in the middle of the stream, he pointed out a rock and told me to squat. I flatly refused. Sometimes you just know when something will not work. I argued against his errant confidence in my gracefulness and the length of my legs. It was pointless; he had found the eight hundred sixty-fourth 'perfect shot', and I was not going to win this one. I straddled the slippery ground and waited for his pounce. His long legs brought him over successfully, and the camera did its job. He exited, offering me his hand for my return ashore. Step one went fine. Step two twisted me in a very wrong direction. Step three made me wish the camera would wash away downstream. As expected, my leg plunged into the cold drink, as I simultaneously banged my thigh on a rock.

The only thing worse than hiking in wet shoes and jeans is the odd sensation of hiking in one wet pant leg and one wet shoe. It was a silent trek back to the car, but at least the goals were clear. We wanted showers and dinner. As the sun set, we realized that cooking was out of the question, but there was a resort restaurant along the road to the campground. It took two attempts to drive into the right campground and shower house… that, to our chagrin, had closed an hour earlier. We were dumbfounded, having never encountered shower houses with curfews. Still, there was no way I was going to bed like this.

Utilizing the ingenuity that only a seasoned and annoyed camper possesses, I packed a small basin, towel, and change of clothes, and headed for the bathroom. Using the soap and water at the sink, I filled the dishpan and carried it into the handicapped stall. Thankfully, there was a baby changing station inside, affording me a 'table' on which to place my dishpan. I stripped down, careful not to touch anything. Somewhere between sudsing my whole body and preparing to rinse via saturated washrag, I heard the door start to open. It was not that I had any particular modesty or dignity left at this moment, but it did startle me.

The door slammed shut immediately, as I listened to the faint arguing outside. My faithful and unilingual doorman was doing his best to convince the Spanish-speaking janitor that he would have to wait to come in and clean. *La chicita esta bagno. No entero! Cinco minuto, por favor!* I finished my makeshift shower, towel-wrapped my hair, and casually left the bathroom, amiably ignoring the bewildered janitor.

Now the rustic duo began their quest for nourishment. By this time it was dark, and the restaurants we had counted on were closed. This is why you should never leave home without peanut butter and jelly. We assembled our sloppy, sticky sandwiches from the cooler in the trunk, while parked under a streetlight that taunted us by cycling on and off at just the wrong moments. After a quick survey for bears, we sat on a storefront bench and nibbled away hungrily. With full bellies and the pleasant childhood memories that an expertly constructed pbj always brings, we drove back to our campsite to try to get a good night's sleep.

We were both very tired, but that did nothing to help us fall asleep. We talked, tried to read, tossed, turned, and eventually gave up: I to a light sleep, he to the idea of not getting any rest. About two minutes into my first dream, Senator asked if I was awake. *Well, actually...* He was ready to move on, immediately. I could relate to his annoyance at the evening's progression, and to the feeling of wanting to get going and move on to the next place. The night was a bust. If he was awake enough to drive, so be it.

We aimed our car south and scanned the radio stations for anything interesting. Once we were out of the forest, the night canopy was filled with stars. I was more awake, and we anticipated the next leg of the trip. After all, how many people do you know who have been to Idaho?

It was nearing midnight, so we decided to get a room in Jackson Hole for the night. To say that this was the most miserable place we have ever visited in the time we have traveled together would be putting it kindly. Every street in the small town teemed with staggeringly drunk college-age kids. The clumps of brain damaged beer containers yelled, slurred, and repeatedly stepped out into traffic at a whim's notice. *So that's why they call it Jackson 'Hole'*. There was no vacancy at the seedy motels, which did not break my heart. No words were necessary; we agreed that driving over the steep mountains in the middle of the night would be less of a risk than staying in boozetown. At 2:00am, we checked into a hotel in Idaho Falls.

Saturday morning marked one week since we had left home and our itinerary called for another eight days on the road. It was time to reevaluate. We checked out of the badly outdated room and found the essential laundromat. While our confused clothes mingled and tumbled in their foreign surroundings, we went next door for breakfast and a meeting of the travel companions, which, like the book group, boasted 100% attendance.

"What do you want to do?" "Well, whatever you want is fine, but..." It soon became clear that we were both ready to head home. Paying for hotels instead of campsites had been an extra expense, and Senator's cold had infested him for four states. Surprisingly, the decision to turn back east was neither disappointing, nor did it feel like a failure. We would not skip anything that we had specifically planned to do; we just would not drag the journey out as long.

With an even number of clean dry socks (always encouraging), we entered the interstate to enjoy the freedom of the Montana highway system. Several years ago, this forward-thinking state did away with daytime speed limits on their interstates, forever earning the respect of safe-but-lead-footed drivers like myself. We did not see any signs anywhere, and the occasional car that did pass averaged about ninety-five miles per hour, so we opted for the 'when in Rome' rule. Perhaps it is relative. The land and sky are so big that it doesn't really feel like you are going *that* fast, so I guess it all balances out. Senator pulled out the remainder* of *The Fountainhead* to check on Howard Roark.

The sunny afternoon passed quickly, and we stopped in Billings. It took a little bit of scouting to find a restaurant that did not specialize in oversized beef, but we eventually found an excellent and very reasonably priced Italian restaurant. They didn't even try to sneak meat into our pasta. The cow is worshiped in the West, so long as it is on the plate. Billboards for competing restaurants advertise "Huge Burgers!", "Even Bigger Burgers!", and "So Much Red Meat in One Serving That if

---

* Working in a bookstore gave us occasional access to 'stripped' books. These are mass-market paperbacks whose covers are stripped off and sent to the publisher for credit when they do not sell. This process is more cost-effective than returning the entire book. The joy of reading a stripped book is twofold: 1.) it's free, and 2.)you can rip off each chapter and throw it away or recycle it after you are done reading it. This is especially satisfying with books like *The Fountainhead*.

Your Cholesterol Isn't Up By the Time You Leave, Your Meal is Free!" Overall, Montana impressed us with its blend of laid-back hospitality, individuality, independence, and ease of use. The larger cities have everything you could need or want, but the entire state maintains a small town feel.

The next morning we continued eastward, crossing into North Dakota. At one time North Dakota wore the title of "America's Least Visited State", which is impressive considering what it takes to get to Alaska and Hawaii, but tourism has picked up during the last few years. Our main objective for being there, (besides the fact that it happened to lay between Montana and Minnesota,) was the northern Badlands. Like the South Dakota Badlands, the northern formations are rugged and host plenty of wildlife. They are even more colorful, and best of all, more deserted. (See top of paragraph.)

We entered Theodore Roosevelt National Park for an early afternoon hike. There was one other car in the parking lot. We toured the entire visitor center in fifteen minutes, and then returned to our car to drive through the hills. When we came to a promising trailhead, we grabbed the camera and stepped out to read the sign.

The warning notified us that we should not hike before noon, as we might get sprayed with some dusting chemical they were dropping to help maintain the natural ecological system of some plant or animal. Did no one else see the irony in this? How did God ever manage before the national park system was there to assist? We stared in disbelief, checked the time, and proceeded.

Though our lungs probably suffered from ingesting toxins in the natural setting, the views were amazing. The occasional lone buffalo looked up the bluffs at us, paused, and returned to the business of chewing grass. We hiked for a while, breaking to relax and talk on the jutting rocks. Our northern Badlands experience closed with another gourmet propane meal involving, bread, cheese, and whatever vegetables were one day away from permanent rejection.

Monday morning we entered our own time zone, and the prospect of home seemed very real and appealing. We zoomed through Minnesota and down into Wisconsin, tapering our speed somewhat in deference to the state's tough speeding laws, but still anxious to cover miles. When evening approached, we stopped in Eau Claire for the night. The quiet exit sported a few hotels, a gas station, and two forms of entertainment. Tourists could enjoy the local dairy and produce market, or the twenty-four hour adult novelty store. We opted for the late show on t.v. that night, and a visit to cheese heaven the next morning.

As you will remember from our love affair with Murray's, cheese is one of our many simple delights, and there was no way we were driving through America's Dairyland without buying some. A huge, brightly colored cow smiled on the sign of the dairy store, happy that milk was the only thing he had to donate to his farmer. Inside, there was every type of cheese, butter, jam, fudge, and other country delicacy that a mouth could want. After much deliberation, we made our selections, placing some in the cooler, and some in the front seat for easy access. Hello lunch.

We then dropped south into the ugliest portion of Illinois. The tollbooths welcomed us home, eagerly swallowing our change. Somehow, we accomplished everything we wanted to, while driving over 4,000 miles in eleven days. We still had almost a week to ourselves before returning to work. We chose not to tell anyone we were home early, buying ourselves a few more phone-free days. The remaining time was relaxed, productive, and gave us an even greater appreciation for our home. Our very first vacation had taught us the lesson of flexibility, but the road trip west contained many new 'challenges' and demands. Meeting them one at a time, and allowing ourselves to make a few mistakes here and there rescued many potentially disastrous moments. Until sitting down to write this, I had actually forgotten how many things went wrong. Ironically, I suppose that is one of the marks of a memorable vacation.

Chapter 7
How I Became Rich and Senator Became Famous: Mid-March 2005

Las Vegas, Baby-- glittering home of world-renowned casinos, white tigers and their very white masters, endless buffets, and a one-to-one ratio of prostitutes to Elvis impersonators. Though not a big gambler, (I could probably figure out how to buy a lottery ticket if given enough time,) I wanted to see it all. Our marvelous country has a long list of cities that have so much personality on their own, that they become their own planets, complete with gravitational pulls. Las Vegas is near the top of this list, and I could not wait to tackle it… as long as I only had to spend a few days there. Senator advised that a long weekend is plenty for anyone who chooses to keep his or her sanity. Despite the recent campaign suggesting that Vegas was the new, hot family spot (from Mickey Mouse to Rat Pack?), I was pretty sure the streets wouldn't be littered with children, so we started searching for cheap flights.

Looking into the third week of February, we were horrified at the price tags on the 'cheap' flights. What happened in the past five months? A few more internet clicks, and re-entering the same dates fifteen times until we could recite them in our sleep, revealed that March was less than half the price. We booked accordingly. Out of curiosity, I called the airline. Was there any particular reason our original weekend was so outrageously expensive?

"Well, of course," the customer servicer smirked, "That's President's Day weekend, the busiest of the year." She sounded as though she were exhibiting a great deal of restraint in omitting the "Stupid." *What about Thanksgi...?* Never mind. We had what we wanted.

We packed our clothes, forgoing the 'casino wear' as we somehow did not see ourselves in sparkling baseball caps and queen-of-hearts patchwork vests. Unlike most of the millions of tourists before us who founded Vegas, we modestly emptied the coin purse that served as our meager gambling budget. I may not know about the travel popularity of President's Day, but I know the odds of winning in a casino. Let us just say the big bosses do not wear Armani suits because the house loses. (Watch for my foolproof tips on how not to leave Vegas with an additional mortgage later in this chapter. You will not win millions, but you will return with both of your thumbs, and that's something.)

We boarded our plane for the lovely flight over plains, mountains, and stunning red rock surrounding turquoise lakes. As we descended into Sin City, the postcard pictures of the famous hotels from the Travel Channel became life-sized. MGM, Caesar's Palace, the Bellagio, and the Luxor's pyramid all came into competing, glamorous view. Unlike many other cities, the airport is barely a few blocks from the action. If it were any closer, the airstrip could double as The Strip.

Once inside the airport, not a moment is lost in introducing the tourist to his temporary new lifestyle. The broad common areas are set up like a mall, colorfully carpeted, with hotel concierge stations where retailers would be, courting your accommodation dollars. The center of the mall is filled with slot machines, and the slot machines are filled with people desperate to start gambling, or desperate to win it all back before their flights depart. At one end of the baggage claim, a Jumbotron advertises the latest shows and entertainment, drawing one's attention away from the beefed up security. We did not mind the extra eyes, though, especially since a rowdy group of conventioneers had already begun their primary alcohol layer for the weekend.

We cabbed to our hotel, noticing that the short ride was not reflected in the cab fair. If you go to Vegas, plan to spend most of your time on foot, or pay dearly for it. Check in was smooth, and all that remained to settling in was the eternal walk to our room. Because gambling is legal on the land, most businesses take advantage of the easy revenue potential. Every lobby is a casino, functioning as the hub of a wheel whose spokes lead to all of the other rooms, restaurants, shops, or theatres.

We navigated our way through the aisles of slot machines to the spoke that included our room number. We and our luggage shuffled down a long corridor, turned right..., shuffled down another long corridor, and turned left. Some point after entering the next township, we found our room. That's okay; we needed the exercise. We flopped our things onto the floral-printed bedspread that was a few months away from passing from 'old' to 'antique'. With travel guides fanned out, we planned our fast-paced weekend.

Friday night was open to roaming. This was perfect as one of my main objectives was to get into the different famous hotels and scope out the décor and design. Fortunately, everything is within about a two-mile walk, so you can easily get in anywhere. It is finding your way out that gets tricky. We wound our way in and out of several establishments, occasionally pausing to drop a coin or two into a slot machine.

87

Here is gambling tip #1: Never make gambling your destination. Simply do it while en route to other activities, as if you were to buy a can of pop from a machine. Moving on, we did our best to avoid the 'card-flappers'*.

Soon we entered Caesar's Palace. The Roman theme is represented beautifully outside, in the classic white architecture. Inside, the Vegas factor goes up a bit. The theme is still carried out, but among row after row of clothing and accessory boutiques. In the recent past, Las Vegas has stretched out its loving arms to welcome the shopper as well as the gambler and the show-goer. Shopping ranks slightly above attending wrestling matches on our list of favorite hobbies, so we bypassed the stores for superior attractions: the animatronics. You do not have a true appreciation for Roman mythology until you see electronic gods spew pyrotechnics and water as their mighty recorded voices reign over you. Our venture into Rome culminated with dinner in its Mexican cantina.

A few years ago, I was sucked into Vegas Week on the Travel Channel. Various programs compared food, entertainment, and behind-the-scenes looks at casino operations, but my favorite was the one that pandered to the tourist like me, who wanted to see the outdoor special effects. Among these are choreographed fountains and a volcano that erupts water and strobe lights every half hour of so. For whatever reason, I deemed it a priority to see this volcano make its magic. The night was cool for March, so I smashed myself against Senator to await the aquatic glory to come. Shortly thereafter, it began to rain, hard.

---

* These poor souls gather in clumps along The Strip with handfuls of cards, not unlike baseball cards, except that they have call girls' pictures and numbers on them, probably with their vital stats as well. They strive for your attention by holding the stack of cards in one hand, and smacking it with a single card in the other hand. The effect is both pathetic and comical.

A strong rain in the desert is not the rare, beautifully natural moment one might suppose. In fact, it is downright annoying when you are waiting for a fabricated volcano to erupt. After several false starts, the speakers, cleverly disguised among the palm trees, announced that the show was canceled. We started back toward our hotel, and then back the other mile to our room.

We got a good night's sleep, which is important considering the pace of Las Vegas makes New York City look like a sleepy village. It was Saturday morning, and there was a little time to kill before embarking on our Hoover Dam tour, so we went to our hotel's casual restaurant. Like the rest of the Tropicana, it was festooned in pink, turquoise, yellow, and many flowers and birds that do not exist naturally within a 400-mile radius of Las Vegas. The food was average (it's eggs, not brain surgery), but our server was pleasant, patiently wishing us 'good luck', for what must have been the twenty thousandth time in his career as waiter. Now it was time to join the other tourists who decided it was worth big bucks to see a wall that held deep water on one side and shallow on the other.

We applied our attractive 'PAID' stickers to our chests to avoid any stowaway accusations and waited in line with a strange assortment of people. There were the usual seniors and a few other couples, but the majority of the demographic were singles. Some looked like they really should have gone to bed at some point the night before. Then there was the single man and woman in the seat behind us on the bus. She was there on business, and he was there because he "was in Vegas every two months or so". *For any particular reason? Mob connections?* I listened to plenty of small talk, and just enough references to each of their families to keep it all innocent and completely boring.* My favorite was the English man who was touring the

---

*Oh, hush-- every writer does it!

United States, from the center point of Wisconsin, on which he was very enthusiastic to share his knowledge.

Our motley crew arrived at the dam within an hour and listened to the rangers give their talk, followed by a fascinating tour inside the dam. We watched the requisite visitor center films, accompanied by the soothing soundtrack of progress. I wish I could give you the stats, but suffice it to say that a whole lot of water and power are set into motion, in spite of the desert landscape. Continuing the full experience of Hoover Dam, we walked across the top to Arizona. (It was precisely half as exciting as standing at Four Corners in the southwest.) Check one more state off the list.

Finally, it was time for the grand finale of any American tourist spot—the gift shop. This is not only the scene of your standard kitschy, crappy fare, but also of the most overused pun on Nevada soil. "Welcome to the best dam gift shop in the world! We've got plenty of dam cool stuff! You can't beat our dam prices! Hope you enjoyed your dam tour! Have you seen our miniature Hoover Dams? You could give a dam!" *Gimme my dam earrings and my dam change and let me go.*

Our good-natured bus driver saw fit to cash in on the literary magic throughout the ride back as well. "Time to get back on the dam bus! I accept any dam tips you can give!" Overall, it is a worthwhile excursion, and we both recommend it; just practice rolling your dam eyes before going. You may need it.

As we returned to The Strip, I decided it was high time we check out some more casinos. The next one that caught my eye was the huge pyramid of the Luxor. The Egyptian reproduction art and architecture are quite beautiful, and the lighting is some of the best in Vegas, if you happen to be an interior design geek, like myself. As I have mentioned, the slots were never so much a destination as an incidental, and incidentally, here is where I made my fortune.

Gambling tip #2: Never carry more than you can lose (including credit cards and the deed to your house, if you are a high roller). While evaluating the Luxor's décor, I was packing somewhere in the neighborhood of a buck-twenty-five in change. That is not slang; I actually mean 125 cents. Carefully discerning which machine and which nickel to pair together, I fed the one-armed bandit. To the amazement of two simplistic gambling virgins, I won $14.00! Never mind the fact that we were spending hundreds of dollars on accommodations, food, and entertainment. I just took the house for 280 times my investment!

I was now a gambling pro, and thus, I developed my 'system'. Everybody who has ever made a bet of any kind has one, whether they realize it or not. They play the lotto numbers that correspond with their kids' birthdays, or they bring their lucky troll to bingo, or, in my case, they know what kind of luck they generally have, and play it slowly, mathematically, and pessimistically. Gambling tip #3: Only play your original pocketful. I moved the $13.95 profit to my left pocket and played my original nickel again. In one and a half seconds, my visions of early retirement and a cottage in Provence vanished. The beastly machine swallowed my coin most unapologetically, as well as three more. *Don't they know who I am here?* If they did, they did not care. We gave up and returned to the pseudo-paradise of a hotel to get ready for the evening's plans.

We started with dinner at an Indian restaurant in the Rio casino. The burgundy and gold gilt theme was soothing and tasteful, yet delightfully exotic, complete with large elephant replica. The food was excellent; cauliflower and okra were never so honored. Opting not to gorge ourselves, we headed to the theatre down the hallway to Penn and Teller's show.

Magicians seem to appear everywhere in Vegas, no dam pun intended. They are part of the tradition. To me, however, white rabbits are from psychedelic rock songs, and magic hats are ones that make your face look thinner. For these reasons, in addition to my love of sarcasm, Penn and Teller were the perfect choice for Vegas entertainment. Their irreverent humor, both spoken and silent, ran throughout the performance, whether they were disclosing sacred magician secrets to common illusions, or simply making good use of gushing stage blood. This is not a show for people who worship David Copperfield, or for those who cannot have a laugh at the expense of Vegas, but you will leave astounded at their many original and masterful tricks, particularly the grand finale. I will not ruin it for you in case you ever go, but I can tell you that it involves ammunition.

After another night's sleep on the world's hardest mattress, we awoke to a sunny Sunday morning. This was not just any Sunday morning. This was not even just any Sunday morning in Las Vegas; this was wedding cake Sunday morning. For whatever reason, your average wedding cake far surpasses even the best cake made at home or bought at the store. The texture is better, the frosting creamier, and the overall experience far more tantalizing. I guess that is why wedding cakes cost more than a groom's entire ensemble. Unlike the previous year, the reason it was wedding cake day had nothing to do with attending another friend's wedding. A coworker had recently clued us in to a hidden gem of the city, called Freed's Bakery. Less than two miles from our hotel, it specialized in wedding cakes... and sold them by the slice!

Let me refrain the significance of this. We could enjoy our fill of delicious sugary confections and fresh coffee without even shopping for a card. To ease some of the caloric guilt, we walked to the shop. Entering the friendly atmosphere, we soon realized that we were not the only goofballs who embraced the motto 'whatever happens in Vegas stays in Vegas' by indulging in cake for breakfast. No one was there to pick up a whole cake. They were all ordering individual slices. When we had sufficiently drooled, chosen, and re-chosen, we ordered coffee (for balance) and three pieces to split: carrot cake, tiramisu, and strawberry cream. It is also important to note, (for those who understand that the perfect cake/frosting ratio should be roughly 60/40,) that the pieces were cut loaf style. Every slice had a frosted top and two generously frosted sides. We entered our sugar comas sweetly and slowly on a picnic table outside the store. If Murray's has a sweet counterpart, Freed's bakery is it.

After a breakfast with no nutritional value whatsoever, but plenty of goodness for the soul, we moved along to the other decadent attraction of the morning: the Liberace Museum. In anticipation of the event, I wore my sparkliest shirt. We walked several blocks until we approached the fabulous entrance, paid our few dollars, and found seats on the piano benches to watch the introductory video. Here we learned about the life and times of America's favorite glittering pianist. Elton John has nothing on this guy. The man was witty, charming, and an icon of unsuspecting mooning females. Sorry girls...

The next section of the museum displayed about twenty of Liberace's famous stage costumes. The man was not in danger of fading into the background. The brilliant and extremely creative uses of feathers, sequins, and layers and layers of silky fabrics sometimes added up to well over 100 pounds, keeping a full time staff of seamstresses employed. Note to self and readers: if you ever happen to find yourself wearing such an outfit, you will need special weighted boots so that you do not tip over on your back, especially if a cape is included. Also, drink lots of water to prevent dehydration.

At this point you may be asking yourself-- although you should know us better by now-- what it was that first drew us to the Liberace Museum. First of all, there is nothing, save gambling, that is a more Vegasy tourist thing to do. Secondly, Senator applies quite the talented hands to the ivories himself, and I, though talentless, adore piano music. Lastly, and far more importantly, we were there on bonified genealogical research. Rumors from Grandma Zuchowski (of Senator's dad's side) told of a possible relation to Liberace. Our quest was not in vain. In reading one of the biographical sections on the museum wall, we learned that Liberace's mother was, in fact, a Polish Zuchowski. It appears that she was a cousin of Grandpa or Great-Grandpa. Unfortunately, this connection did not waive our entrance fee, or give Senator special privilege to try out any of the dozens of beautiful antique pianos in the collection. Who knows? Maybe some of the musical talent is in the genes. This is fine, as long as I never find a furry, gold, sequined cape in Senator's closet.

Mission completed, we returned to our hotel for a satisfying nap on the board-bed. Upon waking up, we dressed and left the hotel, pausing in the lobby to feed the monsters a few more cents. We were a bit slap happy, excited about Senator's new-found fame, and the evening's entertainment. Gambling tip #4: People who are losing at the machines next to you are often not amused that you are having such a good time. Oblivious to their self-imposed foul moods, we walked to the Bellagio for dinner and a Cirque du Soleil show.

There we found a comfortable Italian restaurant, with the best salad I have ever consumed. The entrees were very tasty as well, but it is not often that an amazing salad sticks in one's mind. The assortment of baby greens and fresh vegetables, accompanied by a tangy, garlic vinaigrette, was a perfect meal in itself. Hats off to the bistro for paying attention to an often-ignored course.

After dinner, we walked to the theatre for *O*, one of the four long-running Cirque du Soleil shows. If you are unfamiliar with the Circus of the Sun, they can best be described as French Carnivale meets the circus, meets the ballet, meets the theatre, meets the 1890s, meets the present day. If this is not impressive enough, place the entire show in, above, and under water, and you have *O*. Do not ask me what the 'o' stands for; my best guess is that it represents the shape of your mouth through the entire performance.

The audience knows they are in for a treat when the first scene opens with the actors/dancers rising out of a watery stage. Beneath the stage, the floor ranged anywhere from a few inches below water, to several feet deep. Some performers 'walked' on water, while others dove from two and three stories above, appearing to enter the water only inches away from those standing in very shallow water. The effect was completely surreal.

Add to this the various contraptions to aid the choreography, which often took place in the air over the water. Acrobats swung and jumped from one prop to another with unbelievable hang time that would shame Michael Jordan. We stared at the stage in amazement, and then stole a quick *did-you-just-witness-what-I-saw* look at each other. No human being should be able to do what these people can. My descriptions do not even come close to doing the experience justice. This continued for more than two hours straight, with almost every entrance and exit taking place under water. I will sum up my review by saying that, no matter what your musical or entertainment preference, do not bother going to Las Vegas if you are not going to see a Cirque show.

Monday morning we were still in a stunned fog over O. More and more questions entered our minds as we walked along The Strip for one final time before leaving Las Vegas. We had accomplished a lot in three days. Only a few things remained. I was still determined to see the silly volcano erupt. Since we would be passing by anyway, I also wanted to see the famed white tigers.

We passed the familiar casinos for one last time, pausing for the occasional fountain show. (I kept hoping that during one of the shows, dozens of 1930s-style synchronized swimmers would rise out of the water with flowers in their teeth and ugly swim caps on their heads. I am not sure why; it just seemed like it would have added to the effect.) When the waters produced no aquatic dancers, we proceeded to Treasure Island. Lo and behold, my volcano erupted on time. It was exactly as I (with the help of the Travel Channel and my grandparents' home movies from years before) had pictured it. Like most of Las Vegas, it was deliciously overdone and underclassed, producing a unique sort of satisfaction, known only in such settings.

Now I was ready to meet the big, beautiful white tigers. It has always been my opinion that any cat smaller than a cougar is a waste of time and genetic material. The big cats, though, fall into a different category in my book (which you have chosen to read). Something about the already awesome raw power and freedom of a tiger is further enhanced by striking black and white markings. Viewing these creatures, however, was easier said than done.

For some bizarre marketing reason, Treasure Island aims to attract families. Please do yourselves, your children, and the other patrons of Las Vegas a favor and do not fall for this 'Vegas as family land' campaign. Children poured from every aisle in the casino, which apparently does not enforce the over-18 only rule. Through the swarm of bodies, we fought our way to the tigers' unnatural habitat.

For superstars, they did not have a very fancy home—a few rocks, some shallow water, and a lame reproduction of a cave. I stretched my neck to catch a glimpse of one of the talented beasts. Soon we realized that the cage was empty. After a few patient moments, a keeper came out into the habitat to update a sign that told us the tigers were not currently available. *What does that mean? Are they getting their nails done? Do they have a press conference?* There were clearly communication issues, as a few minutes later one of tigers sauntered into the spotlight, bored by the whole affair. He was magnificent, but the hoards of squealing kids quickly drove us away. This is why I do not go to zoos.

By this time we had squeezed just about all of the quintessential Vegas experience into our three and a half days, and chose to end it appropriately at a lunch buffet. There are two types of buffets in the United States: 1.) the kind that feed very large people the very large portions they require, and 2.) the kind that exist to display culinary art. The MGM buffet combines both types. I halfway expected warmed up leftovers slowly dying beneath sneeze guards. Instead, the many stations offered an assortment of fresh vegetables and fruit, home baked breads and pastries, various international dishes, and of course, enough desserts to make you gain weight just by gawking at them too long. We ate our fill, and then tried a few more things. *No, I did not see the peas-and-cheese salad. I'll be right back.*

      When we had done sufficient damage, we walked back to the hotel to sit by the pool until it was time to leave for our flight. Generally, we pack a lot into our trips, whether on purpose or spontaneously, but the pace of Las Vegas left me completely exhausted. Even though we got a reasonable amount of sleep, the psychological effect of twenty-four hour action, combined with the ongoing celebration of greed and flamboyance, begin to make your head spin. I do not know how people can work there day after day and keep their sanity, smiling as tourists enact the same cycles of hope and disappointment repeatedly. Still, the entertainment is unmatched, and we were not at a loss for a good meal. We had fun and we would go back, provided we maintained our four-day curfew. With these thoughts, we returned to the casino-airport. On our way to the terminal, we dropped a few coins into the slot machines, and won another dollar, bringing our total gambling revenue to +$9.00. Please don't tell the IRS.

Chapter 8
Adrift: Mid-May 2005

The last bit of tranquility I remember before the chaos was Friday, May 6. I met a friend to discuss a book over a pleasant lunch, also sharing my excitement about our impending trip to Alaska, (now whittled down from nine months of waiting to only one more week). I then had a non-eventful afternoon at home, followed by a quiet night with Senator. We routinely popped a classical cd into the stereo and kissed goodnight. Our subconscious states passed another seven hours or so.

And then the phone call. A sullen but hasty male voice asked for 'David'. Before I could get my bearings and decide if I were awake or dreaming, and determine what to do next based on that decision, he interrupted my thoughts. "Please—it's very important." During the seconds in which all of this transpired, I handed Senator the phone, and I knew. Adrenaline sprang him from the bed to the bathroom. Moments later he ran out the door and I helplessly told him to be careful driving and that I would be an hour behind him. Amidst semi-controlled alarm and prayers of wondering how in the world everyone would get through the next hours, days, months, years, I flew into a mental state of preparedness. What physical things did I need to pack? I had better call his work. What do I say to his mother when I get there? Am I family enough to be supportive but not in the way? What if this sinks Senator into a deep depression? Why am I so useless in all of this?

The loss of Senator's father was unexpected and, of course, far too soon. The first few days were the roller coaster of shock, numbness, grief, planning, laughter (yes, if you have ever been in this situation, you understand), fear, and resolve. Mix, then repeat. The beautiful and solemn military funeral came and went on a Tuesday, the only sunny day in two weeks' time. As the angels and saints sadly smiled down on the mortal half, I dragged myself to the upstairs of Senator's mom's house to take a much-needed nap. Lying there, it suddenly occurred to me that we were supposed to be leaving for Alaska on Friday morning. *Oh well,* I yawned. *Tomorrow we will be home and I can deal with the cancellation calls then.*

Senator seemed relieved that I was okay with missing our trip. I wish I could say it was completely because of altruistic love, but in truth, I simply had no energy or interest. The only journey I was motivated to take was to my bed, forty miles away. Though it seemed obvious, we decided to casually mention our change in plans to his mother later on, when we were alone with her. Before we could bring the topic up, however, she took us aside. "Listen, I was talking with my sister and you guys better not even think about missing your trip!" Other family members present quickly agreed.

What?! We began our protest, tripping over each other's words. Here, dear Reader, you must understand the complete futility of arguing with Senator's mom. She was determined that we go, come hell (which it did) or high water (which the rainy month was rapidly approaching). Our two-person army retreated to regroup and restrategize. The more we considered the matter, though, the more it seemed as though it might make things worse if we canceled. With the assurance that his sister would be in town while we were gone, we lamely began to switch gears into a pseudo-vacation mode.

Thursday night we packed absentmindedly and the alarm went off at 3:00 the next morning. My parents drove us to the airport, offering words of encouragement, having gone through the same tragedies themselves, years earlier. I alternated between optimism and looking forward to a restful escape, and sadness and wondering if we were making a mistake. I can only imagine the mountain of thoughts that Senator navigated.

Our plane took off as scheduled, and hours later we were at our hotel in Seattle. Ironically, the sky was clearer there than at home. After nap number one, we wandered the neighborhood in search of food. We found an appetizing Indian buffet. We ate lunch and stared quietly at the people walking by. Following lunch, the uphill walk in the fresh air seemed to do us good. Hearing good jazz coming from beneath the street level, we explored further and found a well-stocked record shop run by one Seattle's colorful locals. Short on formalities and long on conversation, the owner proudly gave us the history of Seattle's prominent jazz culture, playing his favorite samples from the 1950s and 60s.

It was starting to feel a bit more vacationy, but we were still exhausted. We went back to the hotel and did not emerge until morning. With an entire city to explore, we opted for lying around watching t.v. in our underwear. By eight o'clock we were asleep again. This turned out to be the best way we could have spent our time, as we were now better equipped to take on the cruise.

We plodded through the long check-in line, and I marveled that a boat could be so huge and elaborate. It looked like a floating hotel complex. Our ship departed and we watched the skyline float out of view. Familiarizing ourselves with the ship was a treat. Our room was very comfortable, with a large fluffy bed and a balcony suitable for viewing the natural wonders.

In the closet were our life jackets, each tailor-made to fit anyone from 5' 90 lbs to 7' 350 lbs. Wrapped up like a neon orange sack of potatoes, I walked with Senator to our assigned deck for the mandatory fire drill. We made a mental note of which lifeboat was ours, scrutinizing our neighbors. In case we should happen to find ourselves stranded in the middle of the ocean with these people, we had better know a little about them.

Just about the time that I was picturing what it would be like to make small talk with the boring empty-nesters to my right while awaiting rescue, the drill was over. We were now free to relax and roam. We wandered around, scoping out the snack options as it had been many hours since we had eaten. From this point on, we would eat pretty much non-stop for the next week. With this in mind, we also searched for the gym.

As we neared the exercise area, we were invited to join a tour of the spa suite. Sure, why not? Room by room, smiling foreign massage artists and aromatherapists gave their best sales pitch as to why it is essential to your wellbeing that you spend $87 to have hot rocks lined up on your back for fifteen minutes. My favorite room was the 'wrap room'. An unnaturally enthusiastic host with an inflexion control issue explained the wrap process, where he would encase your body in a giant brown tortillaesque blanket, and lie you down in a somewhat warm, soft trough. *Big deal. We've got a waterbed at home with a surround sound stereo.*

I held my tongue; I was being good and these people were just doing their jobs. Besides, it was entertaining and we had nothing better to do. When the wrapper folded the foil outside of the blanket over the portly volunteer, though, I lost it. Giggling, I had to share with the tour group my image of a giant baked potato. Our host feigned amusement.

After several laps around and through the ship, we headed back to our stateroom to read. We were already quite a distance from land. There is something very pensive about a view of only water and sky. Occasionally a bird or fish would interrupt the view, and I would wonder why he picked that particular spot to swim or fly. Why was it any different from anywhere else, and did we interrupt his view? And has he ever lost anyone close to him?...

Soon it was time for our first dinner in the opulent dining room. Months before, when I booked the cruise and the later dinner seating, I was pleased to learn that we could choose a table for two, four, six, or eight. I immediately chose the two-person table, as the object of the trip was romance and adventure with Senator rather than a platform for socializing with strangers. We looked at our dining card and wandered the buzzing room in search of our table number. When we found our table, it was, indeed, a table for two, but it was about three inches from a table of four. What could we say? They had us on a technicality. We introduced ourselves to the couple next door.

Ray and Joanie were a swinging sixtyish couple hailing from a well-to-do section of Connecticut. The situation was suddenly more interesting as Connecticut is my favorite state. Joanie loved the ocean and whales and traveling and talking and Ray loved Joanie's money. This, at least, was our perception over the next week, as we ran into them repeatedly while ashore as well as at dinner. Glancing and grinning at each other from time to time, we enjoyed the unbelievable food and service aboard the Oosterdam, while listening to Joanie's stories and Ray's groaning. The rest of the evening was spent digesting, walking and talking, and trying to process a little more of the past week.

The itinerary for Sunday read simply: at sea. This gave us another day to explore the ship and the view from our room. Keeping the only commitment to health that we had made to ourselves, we started the day in the gym. Even given the very slight movement of a big ship on a calm sea, it was a little strange trying to hold my balance on a treadmill. Nevertheless, a mundane workout takes on new meaning when you are lifting weights watching wild, forested Queen Charlotte Island go by the wall of windows in the morning. Normally I would never be motivated to exercise at 7:00 in the morning, but due to the change in time zones, seventeen hours of sunlight daily, and a week of crazy sleeping patterns, I was more or less awake since 4:00am.

Any good we did was quickly erased by the breakfast buffet. How can one begin one's day properly without fruit, French toast, eggs, and, of course, muesli—especially when lunch is an entire three hours away? We retreated to our room to kill time before attending a nature lecture. For the heck of it, I flipped on the television, musing that it would be funny to find *Titanic* playing.

Instead, I found my newest week-long addiction: The Captain's Log Channel. Move over Weather Channel! The Captain's Log not only predicted the weather; it showed the ship's coordinates and speed, the size of the waves, the expected time of arrival at the next port, and the time in five cities. There was even a map with the outline of our route to track our progress, all set to the delightful tunes of department store jazz. Talk about a geographical treasure! I danced my way over to Senator on the balcony to give him the update. Whether he was actually curious or not, he came over to check it out, bless his heart.

With the vital statistics taken care of, we left for the lecture presentation. The naturalist promptly began, slide show trigger in her hand. She was informative, and patiently answered all of the audience's dumb questions (*Will we see bears and whales? Have you ever seen the northern lights? Do you know where the closest bathroom is?*) based on her decades of guide experience.

We were sort of getting into it, learning about 'calving' and such, (which, incidentally, has nothing to do with birthing cattle). Just then, the slide machine rebelled, and every other photo was introduced with a throng of "Oh, wait, just a minute, I thought I, well, maybe if we, I'm really sorry about this..." On top of the technical difficulties, she was losing her voice. We listened to her unintentional moose impressions, and decided to wander around some more.

We passed through the casino, but my lucky Vegas streak was apparently invalid in Canadian waters, and the boat became a dollar richer. We wandered further, pausing in a lounge for a few rounds of Yahtzee with more breathtaking backdrops. When we discovered that there was nobody in the pool, we quickly changed and came back to take advantage of it. Our floating bodies were reflected in the windows overhead, and I was struck by how peaceful the moment was, despite the knowledge that 1,800 other people were aboard. My thoughts were interrupted by a splash and a dunk, and we swam around like two silly kids on summer break for the next hour.

Toweling ourselves off, we checked the time. It was still early enough to get ready for formal night in the dining room. Wearing our Sunday best, we arrived to Joanie's "oohs" and "aahs" and "My don't you two look splendid!" We returned the complements and got down to the business of choosing an entrée. Ray informed us that we could even have two entrees if we wanted. *Thanks. I think we're good.*

This is a good place to give credit to the amazing staff of servers and room stewards. Not only does the service crew seem to work around the clock, but no matter how demanding the guests are, they always have smiles on their faces. The staff is primarily Indonesian and Filipino, and either it is their nature and custom to be so kind and hardworking, or they are silently plotting their revenge. Either way, they do an impeccable job, without the slightest hint of a complaint. We finished our dinner and took another walk. Each day was beginning to feel like a new adventure in many ways, and we were still trying to pace ourselves. Getting a feel for the time zone and schedule, we watched the 11:30p.m. sunset and quickly fell asleep to the rhythm of the northern Pacific.

Monday morning we awoke to mountains floating past our window*. The air had cooled somewhat, but we were still comfortable with the balcony door open, against the strict rules of the room. We are generally law-abiding citizens, but what is the point of having a door that opens if you cannot sleep with the fresh sea breeze coming in? We dressed for the morning ritual of a workout. Sweaty and feeling energized, we finished and went to find a breakfast table near the windows, as we would be pulling into port shortly.

This was my first time on a cruise, and I was impressed by the intricate process of docking a monster ship. I watched excitedly as we entered the fjords of Juneau. *Hhmmm, we're here about an hour early.* As it turns out, it takes roughly an hour to position the ship in its exact 'parking spot' and to go through the proper paper work to permit us ashore. When the time came to disembark, we went to the lower deck and presented our shipboard ids to be 'scanned off' the ship. In the wake of global terrorism and dangerous underground senior citizen espionage rings, security is tight on a ship.

Juneau, in short, was gorgeous. This is not necessarily the Alaska one pictures, with wildlife roaming the town square a la Northern Exposure. Rather, Juneau is reminiscent of Scandinavian scenes of misty waterways meandering through very steep, forested mountains. In fact, the city is completely landlocked by water and mountains. The locals will tell you that there are three ways you can arrive in Juneau: by boat, by plane, or by birth. This accounts for the large number of pilots living there. Some estimates of the percent of the population with pilot's licenses are as high as 20%.

---

* This is a strange spectacle. When you see mountains on land, there is usually some sort of reference point, like a road or town, which helps you gauge size and distance. It is also a gradual ascent, often from several states away. Seeing mountains of the same height as the Rockies rise directly above sea level, however, creates an optical illusion. They almost look like backdrops in a theatre.

As the capital of Alaska, Juneau offers quite a bit of historical information, making it a great starting point for exploration. The downtown was easily walkable, so we bypassed the junk shops for the museum. The small building housed artifacts from natives, as well as the history of the mining days and Alaska's road to statehood after being purchased by the United States from Russia for two cents per acre.

We concluded our tour by viewing the requisite visitor center film, complete with poor sound and bad editing. The quiet drone of the movie and the warm temperature of the room soon had us dozing. We shrugged each other's heads off our shoulders and left the museum, bumping into Ray and Joanie along the way. Joanie loved history and Ray had nothing better to do until dinner.

Glancing at our Juneau tourists' map, we learned that there were supposedly totem poles throughout the city. The first one appeared to be just across the street and up a few stairs. Now we have navigated our way through miles of back country, as well as the heart of New York City, but various attempts to find the mysterious Totem Pole #1 proved repeatedly unsuccessful. Following the rest of the path through town, we did find the others, which was worth the detour. The brilliantly painted images rose two to three stories tall, depicting representative animals and spirits. Spying Ray and Joanie hot on our trail, we picked up the pace.

Back on the main drag in town, we decided to kill time in the shops until our scheduled flight excursion. Shopping has never been our forte, so we were appreciative when a clerk told us about the library. Not only did it offer great views of Juneau, but tourists could use their internet access for a donation. This was both convenient and funny, considering our local library required everything but a DNA sample to prove that our taxes support them before we could use their services. We relaxed, read, and dashed off a few e-mails, emptying the change in our pockets into the can by the circulation desk.

Now it was time for one of the highlights of the entire trip: the Juneau Ice Fields. 'Flightseeing' is a favorite term of Alaskans, and if you ever go there, you need to spend at least part of your tour in the air. Everything is on a larger scale, and small planes are the easiest way to take in the variation in landscape. Convinced by what I had read about flightseeing, I booked a flight that would survey the ice fields surrounding the city. We walked to the seaplane dock and waited as the guides arranged us in groups of seven or eight. When our merry band was called, we boarded a very small and rickety plane, keeping our balance as we entered the bouncing craft. I have never been afraid to fly, but I admit, I had my doubts upon seeing our plane. The inside of it was stripped down to the essentials, and the bold weight limit sign did nothing to ease the tension. I quickly scanned the group for anyone overweight.

Once inside I put on my headphones and wondered if seatbelts in a plane was a bad sign. I looked over at Senator, who was intently preparing his camera to document what I hoped would not be our last journey. I guess I forgot that a real take-off is nothing like the easy propulsion of a commercial jet. The plane bumped and struggled upward, an airborne Little Engine That Could. *I hope you can! I hope you can!* I was reminded of a story Senator's father told me about another rocky ride in an old plane when he was in the air force… only his had to cross the Atlantic!

Soon our speck of a plane was zipping over meadows and jagged ice formations. From above, the color patterns of the rock looked like a giant striped carpet. The sun illuminated certain valleys, creating shadows in other areas. Deep below, I saw a lone elk trekking over the land. It was truly magnificent. I understand why many Alaskans have no desire to go 'down south' to the lower forty-eight. How can civilization compete with such natural grandeur?

We landed, regained our balance, and strolled back to the ship, contemplating all that we had seen. By the time we boarded, we were hungry and ready for dinner. Preferring quiet conversation about Juneau and other things on our mind, we donned our jeans and ditched Ray and Joanie in the formal dining room in lieu of the buffet. The rest of the evening was casual and restful. We turned in early in anticipation of an early morning arrival in the Hubbard Glacier Bay.

In between the technical difficulties of the naturalist's talk, we had heard her say that the whales would be most active around 5:30am, as we were sailing into the bay. She also warned that the temperature would be significantly colder than the 50s that we had experienced so far. With the sun well above the horizon, we woke up at 5:00 and layered on the clothes. With binoculars and camera, we went outside to the main deck.

Slowly, the ship entered the bay, and the closer we got to the glacier, the more chunks of ice we saw in the water. The air bounced off the walls of ice, creating the effect of a giant air conditioner. Now the water was green, and the ice was blue, together resembling a half-melted slushi. It was also very quiet. We transversed the deck in an effort to see whales, but we only saw one or two in the distance. Meanwhile several seals ventured close to the boat, flirting with passengers.

The edge of Hubbard Glacier was in view. Glaciers top many of the mountains throughout the United States and Canada, but few are active. Most completed the bulk of their activity thousands of years ago. Hubbard Glacier, on the other hand, is in the prime of its geological transformation. The process is called 'calving', which refers to the breaking off of car- and-house-sized chunks of ice. Hubbard is also unique because it sits at sea level, as opposed to thousands of feet above on a mountain.

While scanning the beauty, we heard what sounded like thunder. Curious, we looked in the direction of the sound and saw an iceberg break away from the wall and fall into the water with a mighty splash. The show repeated every few minutes or so, sometimes with several pieces calving at once. The ship settled about ¼ mile from the face of the glacier, and our room was on the glacier side, so we sat on our balcony to witness nature in action. It was such a spectacular scene that it almost felt as though the cruise company had staged it. It is silly, but it was hard to believe that the glacier would continue this process of erosion long after our ship was gone, and probably long after we were gone. I began to feel like an insignificant speck on the sea, and the ship that was so massive in port, nothing more than a toy boat.

As we left the bay, my reflective mood returned to the temporal pretty quickly as we lined up for Dutch high tea. I am not a big tea drinker, but when aboard a floating piece of Holland, do likewise. Senator remembered something he needed from our room, so I kept our place in the line while he ran back. As I entered the dining room, white-gloved servers doled out petit fours and delicate confections for every taste. The miniature tarts and cakes rounded out the tea (which, try as I may, never tastes anything like coffee). The dining room staff, as always, was impeccable, graciously stationing themselves behind my chair every time I made a motion that might suggest I needed to get up. Senator still did not return. *Maybe he's tired.* Meanwhile, I was starting to get excessively used to the elegance and richness of everyday life aboard a cruise.

After more time to relax in our room and another extravagant dinner, we opted to take in the nightly entertainment. 'Barnaby' was billed as a comedian and juggler, which, honestly, did not look like anything to write home about, but we decided to give him a shot. We sat in the balcony so we could make a quick escape if necessary. Instead of ducking out, we found ourselves wondering if he ever played the Chicago area. The curtain opened to reveal a tall late-middle-aged man with long gray hair and a mischievous grin. Barnaby is a very talented and sarcastic showman who grips the audience at their own expense, forgoing the cheap insults. He was also an excellent choice for shipboard entertainment as he was suitable for audiences of all ages. (Normally that description makes me roll my eyes and think of a kid's birthday party, but Barnaby delivers, and he deserves acclaim for his truly hilarious and fast-paced show.)

After we ate again, (which becomes a cruising ritual between just about any two to three activities,) we continued our other ritual of walking laps around ship to get away from the crowds. At the risk of sounding flaky, these walks, sometimes filled with talking, sometimes silent, helped build a significant feeling of connection for me, given all of the questions that still rose out of the chaos of the previous week and a half. We were getting accustomed to seeing the last flicker of twilight die out over the vast black water just before midnight, which confuses the senses just enough to add to the ambiance.

We rounded one of the decks on the stern, adjusting our eyes from the bright lights leaking through the windows to the outside. Facing the wide horizon line, we could see bands of all the colors in the spectrum, like a flattened out rainbow. It took a few seconds before we realized that we were witnessing a manifestation of the aurora borealis, or northern lights. This was particularly satisfying since Senator had never seen them, and I had never seen them displayed quite like this.

Ever since we first boarded, rumors of the best time and place to site them circulated among the tourists, sparking 'big fish' stories. "Well I saw 'em and they looked like giant green ghosts!" "Oh, yeah, and when *I* saw 'em they were dancing all over the sky!" "Yeah, this one time I saw 'em with this guy who lived here, like, his whole life and he never saw 'em that good!" Here and now, the sky was proffering an immense painted horizon, not unlike a music staff, with vibrant reds and violets, soft yellows, greens, and blues, yet it seemed like no one else even noticed. Where were all the Kodak moment chasers now? Perhaps this unforgettable vision was only meant for us.

Wednesday was our second day in port, and we were eager to explore Sitka, where Alaska's Russian heritage is alive and well. In Sitka, because of the shallow waterfront, an ocean liner does not simply dock. The ship settles a half-mile or so from the shore, and the passengers are ferried into the docks via the lifeboats. The parade of little orange boats made us look like a low-budget aquatic invasion.

Once upon dry land, we headed for the town's famous Russian Orthodox cathedral, St. Michael's. Many moons ago, St. Michael's had a fire, and was neatly restored, but without the ornate features that typically adorn Orthodox churches. It was also a bit smaller than I had pictured, but for a light donation we looked around the inside and viewed the vestments and artifacts on display. At least as interesting as the cathedral, is the gift shop next store that benefits it. Here natives and immigrants sell beautiful imported Russian religious icons, hand-painted nesting dolls, and a selection of many other expensive and breakable gifts.

The rest of the town reflects many of the same images, mixed with Eskimo totem poles and the ruins of pioneer cabins, set among a hilly and wooded landscape, with lots of flowers. Because of the shallow, protected inlet, the water near the shore also hosts otters and puffins. Climbing a few uphill blocks off the main drag finds you in the midst a shaded nineteenth century graveyard. This is the true gem of Sitka. The cemetery is so hilly and uneven that stones in the same family plot often sit at different levels, nestled in huge, oddly tropical-looking vegetation. Though the growing season is short, Sitka makes the most of it. Once under the pines and inside the winding paths, one has little knowledge of the surrounding town. While we were enjoying the pace and activity of the cruise, it appeared that we had sought out yet another quiet retreat within a holiday.

As we neared the end of our day in Sitka, we attempted to get one last picture along the water, seated on some wooden planks. This was easier said than done. Though we chose an empty, out-of-the-way spot, someone drove up just as we got into position. We waited. Soon a friend joined her. We waited. Just as we were about to move, they drove away.

Take two. We reconfigured the shot and were just about ready when someone walked in front of our camera. Suddenly our vacant corner was Grand Central Station. *I didn't realize we were such trendsetters.* Eventually we snapped a quickie and left to catch our ferry back to Das Boot.

After a short nap with more contraband breeze flowing through our stateroom door, we hurried to the 'food deck' for an ice carving demonstration. In the midst of an attentive crowd, the lumberjack chefs skillfully sawed their way through two man-sized hunks of ice. I had seen similar demonstrations on television, but I always assumed that the footage was edited down from a project that originally took several hours. I was shocked when, within just about twenty minutes, the formless hunks of ice were effortlessly transformed into a whale and an eagle. *All this watching other people work so hard is making me hungry…*

We again joined Ray and Joanie at dinner, separated by our three inches of privacy. We mentioned that we were going to see the crew show after dinner. Joanie loved the crew and smiled contentedly as she praised them. Ray spewed the facts of how much they were paid, how many days per year they worked, and how well off their families were in the Far East. He continued to expound on the economics of foreign labor pools. I was more interested in the swimming pool. *She could do much better.* Ray then steered the conversation, as he always inevitably did, to the fact that, yet again, we had no meat on our plates. *Yeah, how about that? A whole four days in a row!* We bid our peace to the happy couple and left for the auditorium.

The 'crew show', as it is simply known, quickly became one of my favorite cruise experiences. Somewhere in between working twenty hours a day and sleeping, a few dozen members of the dining room and steward staffs contrived, rehearsed, and presented a variety program based on native Indonesian traditions. The elaborate costumes and dances were interspersed with the commentary of one of the dining room attendants. His offbeat, thickly accented, dry sense of humor was, by this time, familiar to most of the passengers. The performance was a professional blend of National Geographic, an Asian choir, and a traveling comedy/dance troupe, warranting an immediate standing ovation. Walking back to our room, I hoped the crew made more money than Ray said, but I tended to believe he was right.

Thursday morning brought the gray sky and spring drizzle that we were told to expect. In just a while we would disembark in Ketchikan, a favorite cruise port known for its mining history and precious gem and metal industries. Every other shop boasts discount gold, silver, and rare stones. The town itself is well kept, and most of the downtown buildings have the same gray wooden siding, reminiscent of the New England shoreline.

Winding beneath footbridges are shallow inlets of seawater. We walked a few blocks to a restored brothel from the late 1800s. *Now let's learn some real history.* We were loudly greeted by an interpreter who may well have been living out some bizarre fantasy as she played her feather-boaed and heavily make-uped role.

The madam gave us all the dirt on the town's founders, concluding the tour by highlighting the infamous pink bathroom with a curtain made of Victorian condoms. *Well that's something you don't see every day. It probably brings in more tourist donations than the vintage chairs.* From the brothel, we headed for the purity of the local museum, where, of course, we ran into our mateys, Ray and Joanie. They were on their way to the historic house of ill repute. *I could see Joanie as one of those tour guides. She had the big, friendly, buoyant personality for it, and she probably already owned a boa...*

We watched the ships in the distance before boarding again. If we hit it right, we could attend high tea, which Senator missed last time due to a lack of communication and a navigational error (on our part, not the ship's). This time tea was held in a smaller lounge, with windows looking out just above the surface of the water, offering a unique perspective. We situated ourselves at a table in the middle of the room. Tea would not be nearly as formal this time, but the pastries and service would be superb nonetheless.

More parties filed in, filling the dozen or so tables. Soon the staff began serving from both sides of the room, making repeat trips to the kitchen for full trays of goodies. Now everyone had plates of miniature cakes, except us. "They must be waiting for more," we agreed. Next, the tea was poured... for everyone else. *Hello. Thirsty tourists here.*

After several more trips past our table without so much as an acknowledgment, we forgot about the tea and treats, wrapped up in the fascination of the situation. How could they miss us? It was becoming almost comical. Were we on Candid Camera? We started to make a game of it. I chose one server and stared him down as he criss-crossed the room offering the others seconds. Not a blink. We then began talking loudly to see if our voices would attract any notice. *These guys are good.* Amazed, we admitted defeat and walked out, never eliciting a single nod from the people who could not do enough for me just a few days before. Senator maintains that the servers snubbed us because I brought a boy along this time, instead of arriving solo. That is all right. I'll take my sweetie over sweets any day.

As the afternoon progressed, the waves got a bit choppy, giving the ship a pleasant swagger. We were having fun with it, exaggerating our instability when no one else was looking. It did not seem that bad, but apparently it was wavy enough that several people were getting sick. At this point I had two epiphanies: 1.)Why would anyone pay for alcohol on a ship when he could get tipsy for free? and, 2.)I bet the pool is empty and a lot of fun right now! We quickly changed into our swim gear and proved my theory correct. We got more than a few stares from people passing through, but it was perfect. We had the waves of the ocean in the clean water of the pool. After our hearty swim, it was time to do you know what.

We dried and changed for dinner. Scanning the evening's menu, we learned that this was the night of the Baked Alaska Parade. Okay. We selected our entrees and chatted with the now tolerable Ray and the ever-entertaining Joanie. Joanie was excited about the 'parade', explaining the event with sincere reverence. Her tale was not exaggerated. Once everyone had finished their meals, the lights were dimmed, and the parade music began. The dining staff lined up dutifully, each server armed with a plate carrying a loaf-like creation with a creamy white top. Protruding from each dessert were sparklers, naturally. They proudly marched the baked Alaskas (Alaski?) around the room for everyone to admire.

When the route was complete, the music faded out and we were served the delicious cherry dessert. It was now five days into the cruise and the sanctimonious adoration of food was becoming almost sickening. Occasionally the guilt of so much epicurean excess creeps in. *Gym. First thing tomorrow morning.*

We staggered around the ship, noting that the waves continued to increase. This was getting exciting! We descended to a lower deck where we could watch the waves crash in full drama. Why weren't people enjoying this part of the cruise? This was all part of the raw power of the Alaskan wild, too. *Take your Demerol and experience it, darn it!*

When I was rocked off my soapbox, I sat quietly, mesmerized by the water. Senator was pensive as well. It occurred to me that the times when we most wish we could read another person's mind are generally the times when we're not supposed to. I thought about all that had happened recently. It was a bizarre reality in which we found ourselves, isolated from the rest of the physical world, but certainly not from our thoughts. We retreated to our room to let the ocean rock us to sleep.

Friday was our last full day aboard, and we fulfilled our vow of one last day in the gym. Partly because most people had given up exercising by now, and partly because the boat was still rather rocky, the gym was nearly empty. I waited for my aerobics class to begin, but the instructor deemed the idea of hopping around and trying to balance as unwise. *Oh, well. I tried.* I used the treadmill for a few minutes, mainly for the novelty of it. When this wore off, we left to join the other passengers who were testing their balancing skills by carrying trays of food from the buffet. All those years of waitressing were finally put to good use.

Later we would dock in Victoria, but there was not much going on during the day. We glanced over the agenda and listened to the announcements of the perky cruise director. We had bypassed many of the activities, preferring to do our own thing. After all, we had already sacrificed the intimacy of our 'two-person' dining table. Throughout the week, the staff had hosted their version of American Idol, a reality television show that gave wannabe stars the chance to sport their talents, a word often loosely used in said context. Today they were holding the finals. Reasoning that the finals might actually have people who could sing, we ventured to the auditorium.

The two finalists were, annoyingly, a married couple. (Insert your own dumb jokes here. The emcee sure did.) In all fairness, they could carry a tune or two. What I did not count on, however, was that all of those tunes would be country songs, in the twangiest, hillbilliest sense of the genre. Just in case you wanted to play along, the words were displayed on the large screen, stage right. The audience, working inside the frame of vacation adrenaline, screamed, cheered, ranted, booed, and generally made the whole thing hilarious. They were better entertainment than the finalists were. *Good. Now I never actually have to watch the show.*

At sunset we traded the campy flair of American Idol for the graceful refinement of Victoria, British Columbia. There was not much time in this port, and we had booked a haunted* graveyard tour, so we boarded our tour bus as soon as we got off the ship. Twilight is a beautiful time to view Victoria; the shoreline and outlying islands are still in view as the many-lighted roof lines in the downtown emerge. The name is appropriate; English influence is felt everywhere from the neat, lamplit streets, to the Londonesque architecture, to the wild, lush gardens around even the smallest homes. Our tour began in a Chinese graveyard on the shore, honoring the strong Asian presence on the northwest coast. We then drove through several neighborhoods to the main cemetery.

We parked across the street and walked to the entrance. There were mature trees all around, always a good sign. Fighting the temptation to ditch the group and explore the hundreds of ornate nineteenth century stones on my own, my eyes darted around the neo-gothic array. The guide told stories of hangings and suicides and supposed ghosts of Victoria. These stories interested me more for the historical value than the supernatural sensation, but most of the delivery was tongue-in-cheek.

Finally, we arrived at the grave of Emily Carr. Emily was a young Canadian painter and writer who seemed to disappear every summer, returning at harvest time. Years later it was discovered that she visited a remote native tribe annually, gaining acceptance and respect while studying their community and way of life. Her death in 1945 was greatly mourned, with patrons leaving small gifts, often quite valuable, at her grave. She writes of her experiences with the natives in the anthology *Klee Wyck*, titled in reference to the nickname 'laughing one' that the tribe gave her.

The tour made a few more stops at local gravesites and memorials, but it was getting chilly and everything after the

---

* allows the tour company to double the price of an otherwise unmarketable graveyard tour.

main cemetery was anticlimactic. Our bus returned in just enough time to board before God closed the door of the ark. *I wonder what would have happened if we missed the boat. I guess we would just be a bus full of Yankee ex-patriots.* We perused the familiar late night snack spread for the last time, aware that our cruise had ended. We selected a treat based on tradition rather than appeal; we were immune to rich food by now. The lights of Victoria gently rolled out of view. The sea was calm again, and we were ready to go home, first to our room, then back to Seattle, then back to Chicago, then back Home.

Saturday morning we returned to the harbor in Seattle, disembarking in groups. Since we had no pressing plans and we were not flying out until Monday, we were in one of the last groups to leave. We slept in, packed the last of our things, and sat out on our balcony one last time. The only view now was that of an old shipyard, with boxcars piled three high. Had we been able to change flight plans at the last minute, we would have flown home as soon as possible, but everything was booked. As we walked down the long ramp off the ship, I hoped that the next two days would go by quickly. It seemed so long since we had experienced 'normal life'.

Our cab dropped us off at a simple but elegant hotel in the middle of town. We checked in and flopped in the chairs, looking out the large windows. A few blocks north stood the Space Needle, the Twentieth Century's link to the Jetsons. Then our eyes were drawn to the movie theatre next door. Around the building stretched the line of costumed Star Wars geeks, awaiting the opening of the next installment of their obsession. Drawing the curtains on the moviegoers, we lay down for a nap. *Would we ever feel caught up on our sleep?*

Hours later we woke up hungry. Now it was pouring out. Everyone associates Seattle with rain, and it is true that most days there is some precipitation. In Seattle's defense, however, the rain may only occur for fifteen minutes of the day, leaving the sun to shine the remainder of the time. Tonight, the clouds had definitely staked their claim. Carless, and in need of fresh air, we quickly hiked the few blocks to a Mexican restaurant in the neighborhood. Other dripping customers waited to be seated. Apparently other people were not afraid to get wet either, or else they were 'lifers' who probably didn't even notice the rain anymore. When we had had our fill of the delicious warm, spicy food, we splashed our way back through the downpour, looking forward to a dry night vegging in front of the tube.

As promised, Sunday morning started out dry. I was in a more ambitious mood as we walked to Pike's Place, world famous market and most likely place to get hit in the head with a flying fish. I figured the place would be busy, but I did not expect it to be body-to-body-to-stroller-to-body. One pass through the narrow market was enough. Far more interesting are the shops that line the streets around it. We stumbled upon a Russian bakery that specialized in baked dough pocket sandwiches. The employees scrambled to fill orders for the crowd around the tiny counter. Good choice. The sea gulls must have agreed, too; they followed us intently, scrutinizing the ground for any stray crumb.

Finishing our sandwichokovs, we made our way to the Space Needle and City Center. The Needle, ironically, looks far more impressive from a distance. When we got to the bottom, we looked at each other, shrugged, and kept walking, aware that the admission price of going up in the Sears Tower was a fraction of what it would cost to go up in the Space Needle, which is a fraction of the height. We had other amusements on the agenda anyway.

In the same plaza is a newer complex that houses the Experience Music Project (EMP), and the Science Fiction Hall of Fame. We found our way into the Sci-Fi hall first. Yes, Reader, I know you will point your finger and call me a hypocrite for making fun of the Star Wars geeks outside the hotel, but this was *real* science fiction, not a bad Hollywood series. The museum, which takes in several floors and rooms, is laid out like a space control center, with floor plans on the walls to guide the Earthling. This museum deserves dual acclaim: 1.) The exhibits are high quality and complete, and 2.)even if you are not a fan of the genre, there are so many cultural reference points that it is both fascinating and nostalgic. After all, where would our society be without the lessons learned in *The Day the Earth Stood Still*? Among my favorite highlights were Robot from *Lost in Space* ("Danger, Will Robinson! Danger!"), the space weaponry display (anyone seen my ray gun?), and the wall of first edition prints of the early sci-fi masters like Wells, Asimov, and Orwell. If you are in Seattle, take the kids, take the grandparents, and go.

On the other side of the same building is the Experience Music Project. A private Jimi Hendrix devotee founded this museum and center for creativity as a tribute to the rock and roll heritage of the last forty or so years. The museum's centerpiece is a two-story sculpture made entirely of guitars, situated opposite a giant video wall, which greets the visitor with a larger-than-life Hendrix performing at Woodstock. *Wow! I can almost feel the mud!* The exhibits kick-off with "The Beatles in America", complete with reprinted fan letters and letters of complaint about the long haired menaces to society. From here you are taken on a tour of rock music history, with a special focus on Seattle's contribution. (Thankfully, Kurt Cobain has not been declared a saint... yet.)

Another section of EMP is reserved for creating your own video, or experimenting with instruments and distortion effects. This could be entertaining for kids, but don't look for any low-budget videos of a grainy Daver rockin' out anytime soon. Surprisingly, EMP was not as professionally staged as the Sci-Fi Hall of Fame, but it was still fun in a scratch-the-surface-of-rock-history kind of way.

The sun retreated just in time for our long trek back to the hotel. We stopped for java to take along with us. Fun fact: the average Seattleite's veins pump 76% blood and 24% coffee.

There is no shortage of the devil's caffeinated brew. If you do not eat seafood, on the other hand, food can be a bit more of a challenge. We opted to make our last vacation dinner a bagful of selections from a neighborhood deli. "We'll take those salads, and that cheese, and one of those and two of those, and..." Laying out our spread on the standard-issue hotel room table, we passed another quiet night, knowing we would be in our own bed the next night.

It would have seemed like a long and surreal journey even without the tragedy that preceded our trip. To feel so removed from circumstances while trying to process so much is not an easy task. We had talked to Senator's mom almost every day that we were gone, but long distance phone conversations rarely do much to ease a concerned mind. Even amidst the unanswered questions, concerns, and flat-out fears, we found reasons to laugh and create new memories. Though we knew when we left that these memories would always be somewhat tainted in light of their surrounding events, it became apparent that we had done the right thing in going. Who knows? Maybe Frankie was along for the ride.

Afterword

I have always said that any two people who plan to enter into a serious relationship should have to take a trip together first. The planning, preparation, execution, and flexibility involved in travel are all illustrations of skills necessary for life. You also learn how truly compatible you are, especially when things do not run as smoothly as planned. Our journeys have taught me a lot, and they have been an integral manifestation of our sense of adventure and appreciation for the world around us. As I look forward to upcoming trips, I am conscious of my Grandma's simple advice, "Go—as much as you can, whenever you can!"

www.ingramcontent.com/pod-product-compliance
Lightning Source LLC
LaVergne TN
LVHW041630070426
835507LV00008B/543